FREEDOM
FROM THE SPIRIT OF
REJECTION

Receiving the Father's Love
Rejecting the Enemy's Lies

DR. ELIZABETH FONDONG

DR. ELIZABETH FONDONG

Printed in the United States of America
First Printing June 2021
First Edition June 2021
Second Printing August 2021

ISBN: 979-8501695542

10 9 8 7 6 5 4 3 2 1

Editors: Mischka Johnson & Traci Malinoksi

DEDICATION

To the Heavenly Father, our Wonderful Lord Jesus, My Mighty Deliverer, and the Blessed Holy Spirit who inspired every word of this book.

To all who are part of the Bride of Christ; you who wash your garments in the Love of the Father, getting them ready for the wedding feast of the Lamb.

To the memory of my Dad, Zach Fomum, who demonstrated the love of the Father and sowed the seeds of greatness in me.

To my loving husband whose unconditional love for me, releases a harvest of greatness through me.

Dedication to the Heavenly Father

To The Heavenly Father,

The Father's Love Healing River

When you bathe in it, He washes the wounds of shame and pain

When you soak in it, He heals the paralysis of fear and doubt

When you swim in it, He restores identity and purpose!!

Hallelujah, I love that Healing River!!!

By Dr. Elizabeth Fondong

TABLE OF CONTENTS

Foreword 1

By Bishop Robinson Fondong

Foreword 4

By Michael Van Vlymen

Acknowledgments 6

Chapter 1 9

Freedom From The Spirit Of Rejection

Chapter 2 13

God's Original Plan: Walking Hand In Hand With Your Father

Chapter 3 17

Coming Out Of The Land Of Affliction

Chapter 4 21

The Father's Wishlist Beyond Hand In Hand

Chapter 5 27

The Operation Manual Of The Spirit Of Rejection

Chapter 6 31

Manifestations Of The Spirit Of Rejection

Chapter 7 43

Giving Sight To The Blind

Chapter 8 47

Loving God, Loving Self, And Loving Neighbor

Chapter 9 53

From The Land Of Scarcity To The Land Of Abundance

Chapter 10 61

Exodus From The Land Of Lies And Deception

Chapter 11 65

Come As You Are: Gather Around The Father's Love

Chapter 12 69

The "Nobody To Help" Trap

Chapter 13 79

How The Spirit Of Rejection Comes In

Chapter 14 85

Time To Forgive

Chapter 15 89

Destroying The Man-Made Strongholds

Chapter 16 95

Changing Your Spiritual Address

Chapter 17 101

Eviction Notice

Chapter 18 105

"Behold, I Am Doing A New Thing"

Chapter 19 113

God's Purpose For Your Deliverance

Chapter 20 121

He's Looking For You

Afterword 129

About The Author 132

FOREWORD

BY BISHOP ROBINSON FONDONG

"For whosoever shall call upon the name of the Lord shall be saved."

(Rom. 10:13 KJV)

My beloved wife, Dr. Elizabeth Fondong, is a treasure beyond measure! The above verse is the testimony of her life. The woman I call "the most beautiful woman in the world," is also a miraculous woman. I saw the battle she went through dealing with rejection. Her present life of victory over rejection is truly the evidence of the grace and goodness of God! She is a walking miracle!

When we got married, I was surprised to notice the battle for love and acceptance that she craved. I truly love my wife and she knows it, but it was a battle to convince her of my love. She would react to the slightest correction. A tiny issue would become so serious. I often wondered whether she was reacting to something I just said or something else.

My precious wife has always been a passionate lover of the Lord Jesus Christ. Her passion and commitment to the Lord are contagious! I have learned so much from her. But there was always this inner battle of rejection that she just could not get rid of. When we discovered that it was demonic, she was determined to get rid of this demon. Her longing for freedom led to her permanent deliverance. After the deliverance session, I was shocked by the manifestation of the power of God in her life! She was gloriously delivered and the change has been very drastic! The ancient truth remains: *"If the Son therefore shall make you free, ye shall be free indeed."* (John 8:36 KJV)

Dr. Elizabeth is the embodiment of God's goodness. We have four children; Paul, David, Emmanuel, and Anna. Our children have been so blessed to have a mother who is so free and who understands true love. It is amazing to see the difference in her character. It is like night and day! Since her deliverance, I often wonder if she is still the same person. Our relationship has been heaven on earth! The change was miraculous. To God be the glory!

To my wife,

Congratulations, my darling, on a wonderful book. The miracles of deliverance in your life cannot be documented in one book. But the world will be blessed with this book! This book will change the life of everyone who reads it.

To the reader of this victorious story,

There is freedom awaiting you. Your life will never be the same! The great God who transformed my wife will also transform you!

"Arise, shine, for your light has come, and the glory of the LORD rises upon you." (Isaiah 60:1 KJV)

Bishop Robinson Fondong

Senior Pastor, CMFI Miracle Center - USA

FOREWORD

BY MICHAEL VAN VLYMEN

If we are to fulfill our destinies in Christ, walking in the power and provision He has made for us, then we must be free to do that. We must untangle ourselves from the Spirit of Rejection and everything that spirit has done or tried to do in our lives. In this book, Dr. Elizabeth Fondong has produced such a timely message to the body of Christ. We are to reject the lies of Satan and his influences and receive the love of our Father, Lord and Savior, Jesus Christ.

You'll find yourself within the pages of this book as Dr. Elizabeth shares her experience navigating through life under the torment of fear and rejection. Through tangible examples and scripture references, you will be equipped with much needed clarity and revelation so that you can spot the enemy's tactics a mile away.

Having known Dr. Elizabeth and her family for several years now, I have personally seen and experienced the anointing of the Lord upon her life. Her concern and care for the body of Christ, along with her faith and Christ-like character uniquely qualify her to deal with these types of areas. Dr. Elizabeth delivers this revelation with clarity, making sure that the reader knows what to do and why.

I highly recommend this book, *Freedom from the Spirit of Rejection* and I know you will be blessed by it.

Michael Van Vlymen

Seer School

ACKNOWLEDGMENTS

To my parents, Zach and Prisca Fomum: you lived your lives as a bold witnesses of the Father's love. You believed in me and gave me room to grow. I am forever grateful.

To my Husband, Robinson Fondong: the prophet and priest of our home, you called me the Seer of Divine Revelations and the heavens said "Amen!" Thank you for being the instrument that God used to set me free and set me loose.

To our wonderful children, Paul, David, Emmanuel and Anna: you share your parents with lots of people. Your love for me makes me a better mother.

To my Mother-in-law, Mama Alice Fondong: thank you for taking care of the children and many practical things around the home. Thank you for releasing me time to wait upon the Lord and serve His Kingdom with this spiritual truth.

To the women of Arise and Shine: you have all received me as a Mother in Israel, prayed for me, believed in me, learned from me and loved me. I am very grateful!

To CMFI Miracle Center, our online viewers, and all of our fellow saints: thank you for receiving my teaching of the Word and accepting our ministry of deliverance.

To my destiny helpers:

Stephanie Johnson: you took the writing of this book as birthing your own baby! You made it happen, all glory be to God!

To Jaz: your prophetic poem and inspiration unlocked wells within me. To Sis. Teri Charles: thank you for all you do!

To Mischeka Johnson and Traci Malinoski, thank for the beautiful editing work.

To my Coach Susan Etchu: you provided goal setting, focus, and discipline tools I needed to get this done. Thank you.

To my spiritual parents, my spiritual leaders, and my mentors: you have fed me, guided me and prayed for me. I am forever grateful.

CHAPTER 1

FREEDOM FROM THE SPIRIT OF REJECTION & FREEDOM INTO THE SPIRIT OF ADOPTION

It was a beautiful Thursday evening in 1999 when I received a heavenly picture of freedom with which Christ has set us free. My biological Dad, Zacharias Tanee Fomum, who is now in Glory, was, at the time, a very famous revivalist and outstanding prophet and apostle in Africa. He had gone on one of his missionary trips to Kampala, Uganda. At the time, I was 19 years old, in my third year of medical school at Makerere University.

My Dad always had crowds follow him and his ministry wherever he went. He encountered many long ministry lines after meetings for prayers and blessings from the man of God. But this Thursday evening was a spectacular one. After my Dad had given the message, I was running late and I had to rush back to campus before the school gates closed.

As he was rounding up the service, I sent a note to my Dad saying that I was sorry but had to leave right away and that, unfortunately, I would not be able to see him that night.

I had always been a Daddy's girl. I loved my Dad, adored him and wanted to emulate him in every way, particularly his sold-out commitment to the Lord Jesus and to the advancement of His Kingdom on the earth. As the middle child, the fourth born out of seven, I think I suffered from the "middle child syndrome" - never really feeling very special to my parents. Many people commented about how much I loved my dad, and how much my dad loved claiming me as his favorite; he spoke so proudly of me.

Deep inside, my insecurities, lack of self-esteem and ignorance of God's love for me caused me to reject such compliments and continue to labor endlessly for my dad's love and approval. I wasted many years in fear of failing him, not meeting up to his standards and fear of rejection. I missed enjoying the love of my dad. I missed reveling in the approval he already had for me. I missed walking as a special and favorite child. I was working on getting something that was already mine. I was pursuing something that was already in my possession, and

I was refusing to enjoy his love because I did not think I was worthy of it. That evening, the Holy Spirit planted a Seed of Truth that began to shine God's light into the darkness of the deception that had kept me in bondage.

My Dad received the note that stated I had to leave and noticed that I was no longer in the hall. I had already gathered my belongings and stepped out of the hall to catch the bus back to campus. But to my biggest surprise, I heard my father call my name, "Lizzy!", the unique name that he gave me. He handed the microphone to the host pastor and stepped out of the meeting to come after me in front of all the crowd.

He left the crowd to come and see his daughter! I cannot explain how important I felt at that moment, how special! I did not have to wait in line to get a blessing from the man of God. He just left everyone to come to me. As if that was not enough, my Dad took my hand and said, "I will walk you to the bus station."

Hand in hand, my Dad walked me down the street, praying for me and blessing me. I do not remember any word he said, but I can forget his actions as he held my hand and walked me to the bus station. It was the first of its kind. In general, African fathers are not touchy and sensitive as young girls would desire; they are generally very practical and more performance-driven. But here, my Dad:

- left others to come after me
- left what was important to him for what was important to me, making me a priority
- answered my call
- called me by a special name
- exceeded my expectations
- gave a lasting memory
- gave an example to follow

CHAPTER 2

GOD'S ORIGINAL PLAN: WALKING HAND IN HAND WITH YOUR FATHER

"Then the man and his wife heard the sound of the LORD God as he was walking in the garden in the cool of the day, and they hid from the LORD God among the trees of the garden. But the LORD God called to the man, "Where are you?""

(Genesis 3:8-9 NIV)

From the fall of Adam, man fell from his original position of walking in the cool of the garden with God, his Father. God was Adam's Father; he was created by no one else but God. Acts 17:28 tells us, *"For in him we live, and move, and have our being,"* for we are his offspring, as certain poets have said.

As a Father and son, they would take walks around the garden. For example, Enoch walked with God (Genesis 5:22), and Noah walked with God (Genesis 6:9). Walking and talking is one of the activities of friends and lovers. You will not enjoy a walk with a stranger or a boss. The side-by-side position of walking is one that gives a sense of belonging, acceptance, security. Two are going in the same direction and enjoying the beauty of creation.

When Adam walked with God, his Father would tell him His wonderful plan for every one of the trees, the animals, and all of creation. Most importantly, He would teach Adam about parenting. He taught him how he must train his future children to keep the image of God. Each day, these were special moments for which Adam and Eve waited in anticipation and enjoyed. It was Daddy and son time. It was Daddy and daughter time. I can hear Him say to them:

"But now O Israel, [your name] the Lord who created you says, 'Do not be afraid, for I have ransomed you. I have called you by name (just as my Dad called me by a special name, "Lizzy"). You are Mine (activating the sense of belonging and identity). When you go through deep waters and great trouble, I WILL BE WITH YOU... DO NOT BE AFRAID, FOR I AM WITH YOU.'"

(Isaiah 43: 1-5 NIV)

Adam and Eve had received the Word of the Lord to prepare them for the temptation and trial they were going to face when the serpent, the deceiver, came to turn them away from their Father's Love. Unfortunately, they forgot. They forgot the abiding presence of God that was with them, just as we often do. They failed to use the power of the Father's presence to overcome their weakness when faced with the enemy's offer. They also failed to run into the arms of the Father to cry for mercy; instead, they hid from His voice. Surely the deceiver had told them they were damned forever, and they accepted his lie and rejected their Father's Love.

We, like the prodigal son, leave the presence of the Father, and go after other loves. We go along with a stranger who promises a temporary pleasure, a fake and immediate gratification of our flesh. Walking away from your home, you will end up walking into bondage and prison dens. We go places where we will make other connections and attachments that distort and break our connection with the Father's Love.

Luke 15:15 NIV says,

"And having gone, he joined himself to one of the citizens of that country, who sent him into his fields to feed the pigs. And he was longing to fill his belly from the pods that the pigs were eating, and no one was giving to him."

Your Heavenly Father knows what He put inside of you - precious jewels, eternal gems, and incorruptible seed much more precious than gold and silver. The Father's heart breaks to see his children turn down His offer and give in to so much less than they're worth. His warnings are to preserve you from demotion, downgrade, or mutation of your Heavenly nature.

1 Peter 2:9 NIV says:

"But you are a chosen people, a royal priesthood, a holy nation, God's special possession, that you may declare the praises of him who called you out of darkness into his light."

Yes! You are of noble birth, a child of the King of Kings. An unrighteous attitude is not heard of in God's palace. Sin is not acceptable behavior for Kings. Righteousness is how we reign in life in the Kingdom of God. The deceiver has one main goal: to break, wound and distort your connection with the Father.

Chapter 3

COMING OUT OF THE LAND OF AFFLICTION INTO THE LAND OF ABUNDANCE OF MILK AND HONEY

"And I have said I will bring you up out of the affliction of Egypt to the land of the Canaanites and the Hittites and the Amorites and the Perizzites and the Hivites and the Jebusites, TO A LAND FLOWING WITH MILK AND HONEY."

(Exodus 3:17 NIV)

God's own chosen people, the Children of Israel - why were they in such bondage, affliction, and oppression? Have you ever wondered how a child of God can be going through torment and in need of deliverance? Well, the children of Israel needed to be delivered from oppression, hard labor and slavery. They were God's chosen people but in the wrong place. God was sending a deliverer to take them out of Egypt to the promised land, the land of freedom and abundance.

The problem is not as much who you are, but where you are. Remember the first question the Lord God asked Adam in the Garden was, *"Where are you?"* (what is your position in alignment with God?). When man sinned, he fell and lost his position.

Psalm 82:6 NIV says,

"I said, you are gods, sons of the Most High, all of you; but you will die like mere men, you will fall like every other ruler."

Falling and stumbling is not God's plan for you, for He has promised to keep you from stumbling.

Jude 1:24 NIV says:

"Now unto Him that is able to keep you from falling and to present you faultless before the presence of His glory with exceeding joy. To the only wise God and Savior, be glory and majesty, dominion and power both now and ever. Amen."

IN THE FATHER'S HOUSE AND YET IN THE LAND OF BONDAGE

I grew up in a Christian home with godly parents and a happy family. I never heard my parents quarrel, experienced no trauma, and I never lacked anything. I gave my life to the Lord Jesus Christ at the tender age of 5. I was baptized in the Holy Spirit and speaking in tongues at 8 years old. By the age of 13, I received the call of God upon my life; to be a missionary doctor. I had a great head start to life.

ATTACKED BY ROBBERS

"In reply, Jesus said: 'A man was going down from Jerusalem to Jericho when he was attacked by robbers. They stripped him of his clothes, beat him and went away, leaving him half dead'".

(Luke 10:30 NIV)

But at the tender age of 5, I was robbed. I fell into the hands of robbers, just as the man in the story of the good Samaritan (Luke 10:30). The enemy (the deceiver) used his agents, called spirits of rejection, to rob me of my joy, identity, self-esteem and enjoyment of the Father's love.

We had a culture in our home where birthdays were celebrated as a big feast if it were in multiples of 5. So, the 5th, 10th, and 15th birthdays were a big deal. The other birthdays were rather ordinary.

On my 5th birthday, I was anticipating my first big party and celebration. Unfortunately, the very unexpected happened… everybody forgot my birthday; my father, mother, and all of my siblings. No one even wished me a happy birthday. I remember asking myself and checking many times if that day was really the 28th of May. The day went by with no action, no cake, no gifts, nothing special. I mean, what could have happened? Finally, one of our neighbors was the *only* one who remembered my birthday and gave me two donuts.

I waited as evening came, and I had to accept the hard reality that I was forgotten on my birthday. And because of my passive personality at this time, I was not able to ask or say anything to my parents or siblings. I suffered in silence and cried through the night.

The thief and enemy took advantage of that moment of me feeling abandoned, forgotten, and ignored. He whispered many ideas to me, and as an innocent child, how would I have known better?

The first thing he attacked was my sense of belonging;

> *"You do not belong to this family. How could they forget your very first special celebration?"*

Then he stole my sense of worthiness;

> *"You are not good enough; no one even remembered you on your birthday. Elizabeth, you are not as special as the other children. No other child's special birthday has ever been forgotten. All you are worth is two donuts."*

Lastly, he said;

> *"Probably even God has forgotten you. Your parents are people of God, but God didn't remind them of your birthday. If He did, this would never have happened."*

I believed these three lies, and they dragged me from the Father's home into the land of rejection and bondage.

CHAPTER 4

THE FATHER'S WISHLIST BEYOND HAND IN HAND

"Jerusalem, Jerusalem, you that murdered the prophets and stoned those sent to you! How many times have I desired your children as a hen gathers her chick under her wings, and you were not willing!"

(Matthew 23:37 NIV)

"He who dwells in the secret place of the Most High shall abide under the shadow of the Almighty."

(Psalm 91:1 NIV)

"Then the Lord said, 'Look, there is a place near me, where you can stand on a rock.'"

(Exodus 33:21 NIV)

God has a place for you. Your place of freedom, standing in liberty, is THE PLACE BESIDE YOUR FATHER. Under His wings is a place beside Him, far more intimate than hand in hand. Your heavenly Father has carved a place for you, and just for you in His secret chambers. He longs to walk you hand in hand into his private chambers:

- a place of standing (significance)
- a place beside Him (safety and protection)
- a place *in* Him (warmth, intimacy, and security)

Moses stood in that place and beheld the glory of God, God's unparalleled Goodness. Your heavenly Father is calling you by name, meaning that you are unique, special, and His favorite! He promised to be with you, hold you, deliver you, help you, fight for you, provide for you, and give you hope and a future. This is everything a child would dream of from a parent.

I WILL NOT LEAVE YOU AS ORPHANS

"I will not leave you as orphans; I WILL COME TO YOU."

(John 14:18 NIV)

I remember a song from an orphanage, sung by children with no parents, praying to be adopted. They sang:

Oh Lord, please grant us a father, someone who will hold us by the hand.... Oh Lord God, grant us to be adopted, we want to be like other children too....

Oh Lord, please grant us each a father, that's is all we ask of you...

The orphans would sing each night before they went to bed, and each morning their prayers would be answered. Parents would arrive and ask for a specific child and take him/her home with them. Today, the Heavenly Father has come into our orphan world. For the world, since the fall of Adam, became an orphanage. People who have lost their royal identity and their heavenly senses try to solve their "Daddy issues" through every other means rather than going to the Father.

Luke 15:17 NIV tells us of the story:

"When he came to his senses, he said, 'How many of my father's hired servants have food to spare, and here I am starving to death! I will go home to my father and say, father, I have sinned against both heaven and you...'"

Men fled from the loving arms of our Father, our King, into the cruel hands of wicked foster parents (sin, the flesh and the devil). This cruel foster parent took advantage of your loss of identity, your feeling of abandonment, and made you work for their kingdom (feeding pigs). This shameful job and oppressive labor enslaved your mind and wiped out all the memories of the Father's love, leaving you desperate for any kind of attention. And as it is often said, *"negative attention is better than no attention."*

The fall was a fall from the Father's love, a fall from His grace. *"For all have sinned and fallen short of the glory of God" (Romans 6:23)*. Our royal nature was destroyed, and the connection with Royalty broken. The dependence and trust in the Father's love were replaced by an independent spirit and deep insecurity in the Father's love. From walking with God and agreeing with the Father, man turned and joined a new company,

"Following the advice of the wicked, and joining in the company of mockers."

(Psalms 1:1 NIV)

I Will Go Home To My Father

"So, he returned home to his father. And while he was still a long way off, his father saw him coming. Filled with love and compassion, he ran to his son, embraced him and kissed him."

(Luke 15:20 NIV)

The son returning home is just the first part. We must return to the Father. Many people have returned home but have not returned to the Father. But there's **good news**, the Father has seen you; He has noticed you even though you are still a long way off…a long distance away from His warm embrace.

The Father is running towards the son who is walking. His love will always overtake your rebellion. Romans 5:20 NIV says, *"but where sin abounds, grace did much more abound."* The Father sent his Son to die for you, to pay the debt you owed, to restore your royal nature and identity so that you can come back home and feel at home in God's love-filled palace.

The Father Himself is coming to you. He is not sending a messenger. He is coming filled with love and compassion. He is running towards His son, not a stranger, not a sinner. God's perception of you as a son never changed, even with your unpleasant attitude towards Him. Isn't it amazing how He displays what He thinks about you?

I love the story of Luke 15:22 (NIV):

"But his father said to the servants, Quick! Bring the finest robe in the house and put it on him! Get a ring for his finger and sandals for his feet. And kill the calf that has been fattening in the pen. We must celebrate with a feast, for this son of mine was dead and has now RETURNED TO LIFE. He was lost, but now he is found. So, let the party begin!"

HE PREPARED A GREAT FEAST TO CELEBRATE YOUR RETURN TO HIM

He is at the door of your orphanage, calling you by name and offering the ransom for your freedom. At your arrival home, the Father has four special offers waiting just for you!

- finest of robes: royal garments to make you fit and be comfortable in right standing with God
- a covenant ring: establishing oneness and authority
- sandals on your feet: signifying the friendship covenant and walking with God.
- a feast: creating new memories of joy and acceptance.

1 John 3:1 (NIV) says:

"Behold what manner of love the Father has given to us, that we should be called children of God." And that is what we are!

If you read my story and desire your Dad to give you the kind of VIP treatment that my biological father gave me, I have good news for you! One greater than my earthly father is in your midst! He is our Abba father. He wants to do much than that for you!

> *Things To Consider:*
>
> *Will you accept that you may have to change homes, change parents, change identity, and change direction?*

My story was a one-time experience that I have the memory of to treasure, but Heavenly Father is not offering a memory - but rather a lifestyle, an everyday experience, a growing and increasing love relationship with Him. You will increasingly feel special. You will increasingly have all His undivided attention. And you will increasingly feel His warm embrace.

CHAPTER 5

THE OPERATION MANUAL OF THE SPIRIT OF REJECTION

"The thief comes ONLY to steal, kill and destroy. I have come that you may have life and have it to the full."

(John 10:10 NIV)

THE THIEF AND HIS LIES

The enemy steals through lies and deception. You shall know the truth, and the truth shall set you free. When you *know* (meaning become intimate with) a lie, the lie will always lead you to bondage.

THESE ARE BUT A FEW EXAMPLES OF WHAT THE ENEMY STEALS:

- your innocence: sexual abuse and exploitation
- your joy: negative thoughts and fears
- your confidence: low self-esteem and doubts
- your relationships: death and divorce
- your love for God: through love for the world and things of the world
- your identity: through abandonment and betrayal
- your Godly image: through sin and selfishness

Even when the enemy steals he leaves a wound, a hole and a craving. He often posts a guard near his wounded victims to perpetuate and propagate the pain. This is how a soul can be robbed, then crushed and then finally destroyed. After the initial robbery, the enemy will leave behind a lying spirit to continue what he started. **The purpose of the lying spirit is to redefine who you are according to what you have gone through or experienced.**

The robbed man in the story of Luke 10:30 was never helped. Those who could have helped him (the priest and the Levites) never came to his rescue, and if that were not enough, they left him to continue to bleed until he was half dead. It is one thing to be deprived of love, abandoned and mistreated, but when those you expect to protect you, defend you and help you, *pass you by*, the wound of rejection becomes malignant (it begins to spread to all areas of your life).

I remember how the lie that the enemy planted in me at the age of 5 began to grow until it became a tree of lies, bearing many fruits of falsehood and deception. I was a very sad child, very ungrateful, very lonely, reserved and deeply introverted. I had no close relationship with any of my siblings, and I had a very problematic relationship with my mother.

My Dad was like an idol to me. I always loved him, and he could do no wrong. However, I always felt like I needed to work hard to receive his love. With many years of misery and pain as a teenager, I had this little secret that I kept to myself from the age of 5. All my siblings could not understand why I was so different, unfriendly and withdrawn.

For years I convinced myself that I was not a member of the family. I even overheard a visitor who lived with us for a few days asking my siblings, *"is she really a Fomum child?"*. That was it! I had my evidence. I now had a witness that I looked different, didn't fit in and was not loved, although in reality, I am the child who looks most like my mother. I then went ahead and let the cat out of the bag. I told my younger sister, who is many years younger than me how I felt and what I had experienced. My dear sister suffered much from my misery and pain, as I was always so jealous of her. She was the baby of the house; she got all the attention and the celebration of everyone (at least in my own eyes). She had all the things I would have loved to have as a little girl (including a lot of beautiful hair!).

I told her my invented tale of rejection and how I was not her real sister. I told her that my parents (our parents) had picked me up from a garbage bin near the house, where my biological mother abandoned me. The story made her cry and feel so sorry for me. She went ahead and told my parents who, of course, confronted me about the story.

I had listened and entertained the lies that the enemy had told me and began to draw many people to my pity party. In believing a lie, I had become a liar myself.

THERE IS GOOD NEWS: THE GOOD SAMARITAN IS COMING YOUR WAY.

CHAPTER 6

MANIFESTATIONS OF THE SPIRIT OF REJECTION

"For God has not given us a spirit of fear, but of power and of love and a sound mind."

(2 Timothy 1:17 NIV)

The Spirit of Rejection is a mental and emotional stronghold of the enemy, keeping its victims in bondage to the Spirit of Fear. The first emotion that Adam and Eve felt when they fell from the grace of God was fear. They were afraid and hid from God. The scriptures speak over 365 times "…do not be afraid". Fear paralyzes love, but love overcomes fear. The Spirit of Rejection gives you evidence and reason to be afraid. It induces the feeling that you are not safe, and so you must find a way to protect yourself. The Spirit of Fear works hand in hand with the Spirit of Rejection, whose parent is the Spirit of Unbelief.

The Spirit of Rejection's function is to steal:

- your awareness of the Power of God
- your acceptance of the Love of God
- your agreement with a sound mind

The Spirit of Rejection is a self-centered spirit, making you see yourself, your inadequacies, your unworthiness, and your weaknesses. The Spirit of Rejection will offer you a solution to your insecurities, enabling you to create your own Tower of Babel to protect and defend yourself.

The Spirit of Rejection *distorts* your vision:

- of God
- of yourself
- of the world

The Spirit of Rejection will offer you a partnership outside of God and the presence of God, which creates ungodly attachments that distort the image of God in you. These attachments can be:

- people-centered: attachments to the pleasing of men
- physical appearance centered: attachment to looks and the external
- position-centered: attachment to titles and honor
- power-centered: attachment to control
- possession-centered: attachment to things and money
- performance-centered: attachment to results and achievements
- pain-centered: attachment to sickness, failure, and misfortune

- past-centered: attachment to yesterday and limitations
- pride-centered: attachment to reputation and fame
- pleasure-centered: attachment to appetites and cravings of the flesh

All these 10 branches of the Spirit of Rejection originate from a disconnection with the love of God.

"There is no fear in love. But perfect love drives out fear because fear has to do with punishment. The one who fears is not made perfect in love."

(1 John 4:18 NIV)

"Such love has no fear because perfect love expels fear- all fear. If we are afraid, it is for the fear of punishment, and this shows that we have not fully experienced His perfect love."

The freedom from the Spirit of Rejection is a continuous and growing full experience with God's perfect love. The open doors through which the Spirit of Rejection comes in, are feelings of inadequacy, feelings of insufficiency, and incomplete understanding of the **perfect love of God**. The love of God is the Heavenly oil and wine poured on the wounds of your heart, bringing divine healing and filling you up, as for the Samaritan woman in Luke 4:18, drinking of the water so that you will thirst no more.

The Spirit of the Lord is upon me, for he has anointed me to:

- bring good news to the poor
- heal the broken hearted
- proclaim liberty to the captives
- recover sight to the blind
- set at liberty those who are oppressed
- proclaim the acceptable/ favorable year of the Lord

The Spirit of the Lord will uproot the planting of the Spirit of Rejection in you. He says, *"any tree that my Father has not planted [will] be uprooted"* (Matthew 15:13 NIV). The reason why the Son of Man was manifested is to destroy the works of the devil. Seeing the assignment of Jesus, we can describe the weapons that the Spirit of Rejection used to deceive and distort the image of God.

The Spirit of Rejection comes in and manifests itself through these 6 works of the enemy:

- bad news
- broken heart
- captivity
- blindness
- oppression
- disfavor

THE SPIRIT OF THE LORD WILL UPROOT THE ROOTS OF NEGATIVITY

Negativity is the Human Resource (HR) department of the Spirit of Rejection. It recruits all the evil things that come with the Spirit of Rejection: Negative thoughts, negative attitudes, criticism, negative judgments, suspicions, negative words and cursing.

Jeremiah 49:23 NIV says,

*"Concerning Damascus: "Hamath and Arpad are confounded, for they have heard **bad news**, they melt in fear, they are troubled like the sea that cannot be quiet."*

Bad news has an assignment to replace faith with fear. Bad news is a robber of faith and a creator of fear. Even when you hear bad news, let it go in one ear and come out of the other ear. Do not let it spend the night in your house, your imagination, or your thoughts. If you do, it will bring its whole tribe along and take over your land. It will oppress you, treating you as a slave to its claims.

The Spirit of the Lord delivers you with the Spirit of Good News! The Word of God is Good News, the love letter of your Father. "Faith comes by hearing and hearing by the Word of God." (Romans 10:17).

"Anxiety weighs down the heart, but a kind word cheers it up."

(Proverbs 12:25 NIV)

"Death and life are in the power of the tongue: and those who love it will eat its fruit."

(Proverbs 18:21 NIV)

> *"Heaviness of heart, worry, anxiety, fear, and sorrow are all negative emotions that are associated with the Spirit of Rejection. The source of these negative emotions are a negative word that you heard and believed, resulting from an incomplete awareness of the Love of God."*

Heaviness of heart, worry, anxiety, fear, and sorrow are all the negative emotions associated with the Spirit of Rejection. The source of these negative emotions is a negative word that you heard and believed, resulting from an incomplete awareness of the Love of God.

A DISTORTED BODY IMAGE

In my teenage years, I suffered mentally from the Spirit of Rejection, manifesting as a distorted body image. I did not like myself. I did not like my face nor my looks. I compared myself with many other young girls, and I always lacked in one thing or another. Sometimes I wanted God to make me a little taller; other times I wished I was a little shorter. I was just constantly not content with the body that God had given me.

How did this come about? One day my cousin was looking at my picture, and, although I knew he was joking, he said I looked like a "chimpanzee." Can you imagine a more insensitive thing for a 15-year-old young man to say to an 8-year-old girl?

I was shocked but said nothing and began to suffer in silence. I took that negative word I heard as gospel truth. I spent many hours in the mirror asking God why he made me so unattractive, and if he could just take this face away and give me another one. I went through a lot of torment.

REFLECTIONS

1. What are those negative words you heard and believed that are contrary to God's image in you?
2. What are those words you said to yourself **about** yourself, that are prophesying doom over your destiny?

FEARFULLY AND WONDERFULLY MADE

"I praise you because I am fearfully and wonderfully made; your works are wonderful; I know that full well."

(Psalm 139:14 NIV)

"Fearfully made" means you were made with great reverence and heartfelt interest. God saw everything he made in you and said it was very good. "Wonderfully" means to be made uniquely, filled with wonder, and set apart.

I pray you begin to see yourself through the mirror of God's Word and destroy the lying mirrors that speak unworthiness to you and your appearance. *"For as a man thinks in his heart, so is he."* (Proverbs 23:7 NKJV). If beauty is in the eye of the beholder, then you can change your looks by seeing them through God's eyes.

Above all, let us redefine *true beauty.* The Word of God says, *"Your beauty should not come from outward adornments, such as elaborate hairstyles and wearing of gold jewelry or fine clothing. It should rather be that of your inner self, the unfading beauty of a gentle and quiet spirit, which is of great worth in God's eyes."* ((1 Peter 3:3-4 NIV). I once heard the Holy Spirit tell me, *"If you do not like your physical appearance, you criticize your Maker, for you are the work of His hands."*

But if you do not like yourself, then let God change your old self and give you a bright new heart and life. Be born again!

"Therefore, if anyone is in Christ, the new creation has come. The old has gone; the new is HERE!"

(2 Corinthians 5:17 NIV)

It is time to get rid of some old ideas and perspectives and get some new ways to think, straight from God's Word!

REFLECTIONS

1. Do you know that God's work in you is wonderful?
2. Do you see yourself as wonderfully made?
3. Do you celebrate what God has made and not boast about your physical appearance?
4. Do you know your body is the temple of God; everyone who destroys it with neglect, sin and defilement will be destroyed?
5. Do you prioritize your physical appearance over your inner self and beauty, causing a disconnection from the flow of God's love through you?
6. Do you appreciate the beauty in others without wishing to be like them?
7. Do you compare your physical appearance with others and feel inadequate?
8. Have you heard and believed negative comments about your looks from family, friends or people you trusted in?

9. Do you suffer from a disfiguring disease, handicap or malfunction, that constantly tells you that you are not like others, so you're not good enough?

Take some time now to kick negativity and all its ramifications. Jesus on the cross carried all our sorrow, even bore our disfigurement, so that we can bear His glory and see His Glory inside of us.

HEALING THE BROKEN HEARTED

"A cheerful heart is good medicine, but a crushed spirit dries up the bones."

(Proverbs 17:22 NIV)

A crushed spirit comes from:

*   crushed dreams (divorce, miscarriages, accidents, death of loved ones)
*   crushed hopes and expectations (financial loss, relationship conflicts)
*   crushed will (sexual, physical, and mental abuse and violations)
*   crushed heart (abandonment and betrayal)
*   crushed opportunity (disfavor and hardships)
*   crushed love (love not reciprocated)

These are the wounds that Jesus came to bind. His love provides heavenly wound care. When He heals, there will be no trace of the injury and the loss you experienced.

CHAPTER 7

GIVING SIGHT TO THE BLIND

In the story of Blind Bartimaeus:

"'What do you want me to do for you?' Jesus asked him. The blind man said, 'Rabbi, I want to see.'"

(Mark 10:51 NIV)

His blindness rendered him restricted, and limited him to how much he could enjoy of the world around him. He could hear that it was Jesus, but he could not see His face. The blind man knew his name, but he had never seen his face, the reflection of his true image.

He was surrounded by goodness but could not enjoy it. Blindness, particularly spiritual, keeps you imprisoned, away from the wonders of your Loving Father. Spiritual blindness makes you a prisoner to yourself and to your limited view of the world. Spiritual blindness is like walking in the dark with your lamp turned off. Or walking in a beautiful garden with a blindfold on. Spiritual blindness dims you to your purpose, your value, and your worth.

The Spirit of Rejection turns *off* the light of your purpose, your ability and your value. It turns *on* the light of your shame, pain, loss, inability and worthlessness. The Spirit of Rejection turns *off* the light of the goodness and the greatness of God and turns *on* the light of the goodness and the greatness of man (yourself or others). The Spirit of Rejection will lead you astray from the Father's house and to the "pig's pen".

> *"This is what the LORD says; 'cursed are those who put their trust in mere humans, who rely on human strength, and turn their hearts away from the LORD.'"*
>
> *(Jeremiah 17:5 NIV)*

LORD, I WANT TO SEE

Because of my blindness to God's personal love for me, the Spirit of Rejection turned my eyes to depend on, and trust in man more than I trusted in God. I was more attached to the opinion of man than the opinion of God. Pleasing man is a stronghold that leads to many hypocritical tendencies including fear of confrontation, fear of correction and emotional misery beyond words.

As a high school student, I missed so many opportunities, including the lives I would have impacted for the Lord, because of my lack of confidence, low self-esteem, shyness and fear. I had a strong private life with the Lord, as I religiously followed all the standards of our congregation. People looked up to me as the "model child." Deep inside however, I was suffering- struggling to please God and to win His favor. At the same time, I was hindered in demonstrating my love for him, especially in front of my schoolmates.

The Holy Spirit would often impress my heart to share the gospel with my classmates, but I was so shy, so afraid that they would reject me. Even though they all knew I was saved because I did not join them in sin, I never let them join me in the light because my lamp was often times under the basket of the fear of rejection. Being a teenager at the time, my classmate's acceptance was what I was seeking.

I was very sad and withdrawn. I doubted any of them would ever desire to be like me. The enemy would torment me with feelings of further unworthiness, and when I failed to obey the Holy Spirit and witness to my classmates, the guilt of *do you really love God? How come you cannot even obey a simple command?"* would flood my mind. This pain was worse than the pain of trying to fit in. I then created a man-made system to buffer the shame, with more "righteous" acts at church and much more sacrificing, like fasting and prayer. It made me feel better within myself.

This is how the Spirit of Religion works hand-in-hand with the Spirit of Rejection and turns men's hearts further away from the Father's love. I did not shine the light; I hid it under a bushel. I was more comfortable sharing the gospel with strangers on the street than with my classmates who knew me and saw me every day. **The Spirit of Rejection leads people into a double life, and a double mind.** One life where you are on fire for God at church, and another life where, like Peter, you are saying, "I do not know that man" so as to fit in with people.

> *"The spirit of rejection leads people into a double life, and a double mind."*

By the grace of God, when the Lord Jesus set me free from the Spirit of Rejection, the first thing that fell off was the stronghold of pleasing men and seeking the approval of men. I was free! Free to say *"No, I am sorry I will not be able to help you"*, *"I cannot attend your event"*, *"I am sorry, but I did not mean to hurt you"*. I was free from the need to give a detailed explanation and extended apologies and constantly feeling that I could have done better. Free from overworking myself to make others comfortable. Free to love myself and not feel guilty about it. I was free; I am free; thank God I am free at last!

CHAPTER 8

"And you must love the Lord your God with all your heart, all your soul, and all your strength. The second is equally important: 'love your neighbor as yourself.' No other commandment is greater than these."

(Mark 12:30 NIV)

"And so, we know and rely on the love God has for us. God is love. Whoever lives in love lives in God and God in them."

(1 John 4:16 NIV)

The first commandment is to love God with all your heart and all your soul and all your strength because He is the source from which all true love flows. You will not know how to love yourself until you have learned to love God. You will not know how to love your neighbor until you have learned love God.

> *"Some people are givers and will pass as very generous people, but if the wound of the fear of rejection has not been dealt with, these people generally feel compelled to give, feeling guilty if they do not have anything to give."*

However, no man can love God in his own ability. We must rely completely on the love of God to love God. Actually, trusting in God's love, and relying *fully* on God's love is the acceptable demonstration of your love for God. God's love must first fix *your* brokenness and heal *your* heart; then, you can give people a love that does not break you in the process, or cause brokenness in others. The love of God is complete, abundant and falls short of nothing.

Human love, even at its best, is short of the ability to make anyone complete. Human love leaves the giver discontent because it takes the giver further away from God, the source of Love!

Some people are givers and will pass as very generous people, but if the wound of the fear of rejection has not been dealt with, these people generally feel *compelled* to give, feeling guilty if they do not have anything to give, "robbing Peter to pay Paul", and many other unhealthy love patterns. This broken kind of love usually results in giving with no appreciation, giving to the wrong people, and often times being taken advantage of because of your generosity.

The wound of rejection, bleeding for love, identity, and purpose, releases a smell that attracts predators, perpetrators, liars and wolves in sheep's clothing. They take advantage of the victim and lead to further bondage. All these are the associated activities of the Spirit of Rejection.

But Jesus came to set the captives free! Your bondage has sent a signal to heaven for your release. As you read further, you will see how your Father – Abba Father- comes to restore the years that the cankerworm has eaten! He is the restorer of breaches, and the rebuilder of every ruined and desolate place! Hallelujah!

THE LORD JESUS RESTORED MY SIGHT

I used to be like the blind man at Bethsaida (Mark 8:22-25) who needed a second touch. I had received Jesus as my Savior, who forgave all my sins, and I was saved. But I had not received Him as the one who heals all my diseases, particularly my emotional and mental diseases. I had not received him as the Father who wants to hold my hand and walk with me in full display of all men. Glory be to God for His endless compassion for me!

After my deliverance from rejection, I began to see all things differently. Even the sky and the clouds had never been so beautiful! I used to pass by flowers and not notice their color nor the artistry of our Maker. In May 2008, I looked at myself for the first time after my deliverance and said: "Lord God, you did a good job, this such a beautiful face…"

I was most in awe of the scales that fell off the Word of God. The Bible became a living book, full of revelation and light. I cannot thank God enough for my deliverance. I said to my husband, *"you don't know how much you are in bondage until you are set free."* Because of how much we get used to our bondage, unfortunately, it gets to be part of us. But not anymore!

> *"My crooked image of God was straightened, and I met a Loving Father, who was proud of me just because I am His daughter, and not based on my accomplishments."*

There is a new you about to be released, released from the Spirit of Rejection into the Spirit of Adoption! The wonderful Lord Jesus restored my sight with the light of His Love. Once I was blind, but now I see. My crooked image of God was straightened, and I met a Loving Father, who was proud of me just because I am His daughter, and not based on my accomplishments.

The crooked image of my physical appearance was corrected by His love. My distorted idea of submission to authority was mended by His acceptance. My dependence on myself and on the opinion of men was replaced by an increasing and growing reliance on God and His constant love for me. The loneliness and shyness were blown away by the warmth of the Father's companionship. I was released to make friends, give love and receive love.

FREE TO RECEIVE LOVE

One of the prison doors that the Spirit of Rejection had me trapped in was the inability to receive love. I always wanted to be on the giving end. I struggled with receiving compliments, and used to constantly downplay the compliments, or give an excuse as to why anyone will give a good report about me.

I had an extremely hard time with my husband calling me the *"most beautiful woman in the world"*. I felt like he was putting me on a pedestal that I did not belong on. I was afraid that people would look at me because of his compliments and notice how untrue his boasting of his wife is. I also felt unworthy of that kind of love and attention.

When we first got married, I would pray that he would stop giving me so many verbal compliments and so much attention. And yet, on the inside, I could not stand him ignoring me, or his disapproval of any kind, which would trigger a terrible feeling of worthlessness and rejection.

Thanks be to the Lord Jesus for setting me free! I now have a totally new perspective on praise and honor. God the Father and His Son chose to come live inside of me, so I am worthy! I am accepted! I am valuable, and I am loved by the most important person in the universe! Beloved, so are you!!!

"The Lord is on my side: I will not be afraid. What can man do to me?"

(Psalm 118:6 NIV)

How exciting was it to know that God is on my side? This means He agrees with me, He believes in me, He defends me, and He accepts me! What can man do to me?

Man's approval or disapproval has no significant bearing when the Creator of Heaven and Earth has spoken. God is on your side! I pray that you get this liberating light and truth that sets you free to choose God's side:

- God's side of the story
- God's side about your value and worth
- God's side about your image and importance
- God's side about your yesterday, today and tomorrow

CHAPTER 9

"And I have promised to bring you up out of your misery in Egypt, into the land of the Canaanites, Hittites, Amorites, Perizzites, Hivites and Jebusites to a land flowing with milk and honey."

(Exodus 3:17 NIV)

"I have promised to rescue you from your oppression in Egypt. I promised that I will bring you up out of the land of the affliction of Egypt" (Exodus 3:17 NIV). This is God's promise for you.

God will bring you out of bondage. To the Israelites, it was physical bondage, affliction and misery. For most people today, it is emotional pain, mental bondage and relationship misery.

When God saves us and rescues us, He always changes our address so that the enemy has a hard time locating us. He promised to change the physical address of the children of Israel. Today, he changes our spiritual address, our mental status and our emotional residence.

> *Colossians 1:13 NIV says, "He has delivered us (freed us) from the power of darkness, and transferred us into the kingdom of his beloved Son..."*

> "When God saves us and rescues us, He always changes our address, so that the enemy has a hard time locating us."

After my deliverance from the Spirit of Rejection, I felt that I was in a brand-new place, even though physically, I was at the same address. Everything around me looked different - much brighter than before, and what I considered an impossible task now seemed very reasonable. The things around me had not changed, but I had changed; my blindfold had been removed. The Father's love had relocated me from of the land of misery, scarcity and lack to a land of abundance- God's abundant love.

The story of Mephibosheth as told in 2 Samuel 9:1-13 says:

"David asked, is there anyone still left of the house of Saul to whom I can show kindness for Jonathan's sake? Now there was a servant of Saul's household named Ziba; they summoned him to appear before David,.Ziba answered the king, 'There is still a son of Jonathan; he is lame in both feet.' 'Where is he?' The king asked. Ziba answered. 'He is at the house of Makir, son of Ammiel, in Lo Debar'. 'Don't be afraid, David said to him, for I will surely show you kindness for the sake of your Father Jonathan. I will restore you all the lands that belonged to your grandfather Saul, and you will always eat at my table'. So, Mephibosheth dwelt in Jerusalem, for he did eat continually at the king's table, and he was lame on both feet."

THE IMPORTANCE OF NAMES

Your name is what people call you or what you call yourself.

"And Jonathan, Saul's son, had a son that was lame on his feet. He was five years old when tidings came to Saul and Jonathan out of Jezreel, and his nurse took him up and fled: and it came to pass, as she made haste to flee, that he fell and became lame. And his name is Mephibosheth."

(2 Samuel 4:4 NIV)

Let's look at some of the names in the passage above and the Hebrew meaning of the names.

Mephibosheth: "from the mouth of shame", "image- breaker", "destroyer"

Lo-debar: "no word", "nothing", "lacking in good pasture", "insignificant", or "nothing town"

Jerusalem: "completeness", "wholeness."

---

*"Thus says the Lord, I have returned to Zion, and will dwell in the midst of Jerusalem and Jerusalem shall be called **the city of truth**; and the mountain of the Lord of Hosts, the holy mountain." (**Zechariah 8:3 NIV**)*

ENTER JERUSALEM, THE CITY OF TRUTH

If Jerusalem is the City of Truth, it means that every other place is the City of Lies and Deception. The City of Truth has headquarters for completeness and wholeness. The City of Truth is where the heavenly Father invites you to dwell and sit at His table of complete acceptance every day.

John 8:32 NIV says,

"For if you embrace the truth, it will release true freedom into your lives."

King David took Mephibosheth from Lo-debar, the land of nothingness, and brought him to Jerusalem, the Land of completeness. King David did not let Mephibosheth build his own house and live on his own. Nor did he tell him that he is free to visit the palace whenever he wanted, even though either of those would have been a great offer for anyone who found themselves in the position of Mephibosheth. Instead, the king brought him into his own house saying, "Come to my palace, eat with me, learn how you should behave like the son of a king."

God's presence is the only place where freedom can be maintained and enjoyed. Outside of the table of the Lord, you will fall right back into the land of lies and deception. John 15:26 KJV says "*But when the Comforter is come, whom I will send unto you from the Father, even the Spirit of Truth, which proceeds from the Father, He shall testify about me*".

- The City of Truth is a Person
- The City of Truth is the Spirit of Truth
- The Spirit of Truth is the Comforter, Helper, Teacher

This is how the City of Truth becomes the Land of Completeness. Come into the land of Truth, flowing with the abundant milk of God's word and Truth. Come into the Father's garden, running with rivers of honey to sweeten your soul. Enter the Father's City of Truth you will find the exit door to the Land of Rejection and Bondage.

The heavenly Father has a seat for you at the table of His Tender Love. He has a banquet laid out to celebrate your return. He looks forward to displaying how important you are to Him.

I love this song by *Leeland* that says:

"I was carried to the table, seated where I don't belong. I was carried to the table, swept away by his love. And I don't feel my brokenness anymore, when I am seated at the table of the Lord. I am carried to the table, the Table of the Lord."

Revelation 3:20 NIV reads,

*"Behold, I am standing at the door, knocking. If your heart is open to hear my voice and you open the door within, **I will come into you and feast with you, and you will feast with me.**"*

Taking your place at the table is so precious to the heavenly Father because that is the place where He gets to see your face and says, "my child, I love you".

YOUR SEAT AT THE TABLE

Your seat at the table is a seat of:

- sound-mindedness: the Father has placed love, power and a sound mind on your seat. (2 Timothy 2:17)
- enjoyment: the Father wants you to have and enjoy life more abundantly. (John 10:10)
- acceptance: you are accepted and beloved. (Ephesians 1:6)
- trust: the Father trusts you and gives you the ability to trust Him. (Proverbs 3:5)

SIT ON YOUR SEAT WITH CONFIDENCE

You do not choose that seat of honor. That seat was given to you by the Father Himself, the owner of heaven and earth! The Father knows you have been on a long journey, carrying too much extra baggage of fear, doubt and unbelief.

The first thing He would like you to do is:

- Rest: rest from your labor. Come to me all you who labor and are heavy laden, and I will give you rest. (Matthew 11:28)

The next thing the Father would like you to do is:

- Rejoice: rejoice in the Lord always, and again I say rejoice. (Philippians 4:4)

Why Rejoice?

The Father wants you to rejoice because you are a VIP (very important person). But I like to use the term VIP as meaning very *intimate* person. You are important to the Father because you are intimate with Him.

> *"Look with wonder at the depth of the Father's marvelous love that he has lavished on us! He has called us and made us his very own beloved children."*

> *(1 John 3:1 NIV)*

You are VIP because you are loved by a Father who is the MIP (most important person) of the world.

The Father invites you to His table to share His:

- ideas, thoughts, plans and vision board
- training on royal etiquette and kingship attitudes
- love and faithfulness that endures forever

CHAPTER 10

THE "WHY ME?" TRAP

"Why me?" is a common road in the Land of Bondage. It has many billboards inviting wounded and hurting people to come explore who and what is responsible for their pain. "Why me?" will never lead you to the hospital or to the wellness clinic. It will give you man-made reasons why the pain you are experiencing today is your way of life. "Why me?" will tell you that no one understands, and no one can help you. "Why me?" will throw a party called, the Feast of Self- Pity – which is usually made up of the Spirit of Rejection, the fear of rejection, the Spirit of Shame, blame and accusation. The overall overseer of the party is the Spirit of Defeat and Discouragement.

MEPHIBOSHETH WAS CRIPPLED

I can only imagine what could have gone through his mind. *"Why me? Of all Jonathan's children, princes, handsome and impressive, I am the crippled one. Why did God make me crippled? Why did God allow me to be crippled"?* Generally, when men fail to find answers to life's complexities, they easily resort to blaming God.

A KING'S SON, BUT CRIPPLED

He was crippled in both feet. Not just one foot, assuming he could have been able to use the other foot. His crippling caused the servant Ziba to take him to the land of Lo-Debar, the land of nothingness and scarcity. The events around his birth and childhood set him up for bondage, shame and abandonment.

His identity, who he was, and who his father was, caused David to save him and bring him to the king's table. David loved him and accepted him for who he was without stumbling on what he did not have (feet). Mephibosheth's physical condition, limitations, and impediments had no bearing on the king's love and commitment to him.

In this story, King David (representing the Heavenly Father) took this crippled man in as his own son because of Jonathan. It was not out of pity or his condition; it was instead out of commitment to his covenant.

The Heavenly Father takes you in, in whatever crippled (disabled, dysfunctional) state you are in because of his covenant with

His Son Jesus. If you are a child of God, Jesus adopted you, and the Father honors the covenant He has with Jesus and all His offspring, including you.

It does not matter what state you find yourself in, be it crippled or dysfunctional:

- Spiritually crippled
- Emotionally unstable
- Relationally dysfunctional
- Academically disabled
- Appearance challenged
- Financially limited
- Destiny and purpose disoriented

These are things that happened *to* you, but they do not define *who* you are! *Who* you are is who your Heavenly Father says you are, and He says that you are His! The Heavenly Father is your redeemer. He alone has the ability to take the broken pieces of your life and make a completely new life out of it.

"All those who were in distress or in debt or discontented gathered around him, and he became their commander. About four hundred men were with him" (then others began coming, men who were in trouble, or in debt who were discontented).

(1 Samuel 22:2 NIV)

> *"If you know who you are you, will know what tribe you belong to and who can safely gather around."*

These men formed an army around David, they were the Mighty men of David. David started his army with men who had many dysfunctions and disabilities. He was focused on who they were and not what they had been through. The most important thing is knowing who you are. If you know who you are, you will know what tribe you belong to and who can safely gather around.

These men, despite their problems, knew how to recognize a king, and they gathered around David. These men, in their brokenness, did not gather around some broken or discontented king. They gathered around David, who was living in Jerusalem, the land of wholeness and completeness. Like the wise men who followed and worshipped Jesus, even when he was a baby in the manager.

The enemy uses your brokenness, your losses, and your defeat against you. He makes what you have been through to be more important than who you are. The enemy causes you to make decisions based on what you have been through. He leads you into the path of like-minded broken people, which only results in multiplied brokenness.

CHAPTER 11

I tried for many years to fix my brokenness inside; I was so timid and fearful. I wanted God to use me, but how could He use me with this impediment of low self-esteem, low value of myself, and low acceptance of the love of the Father. I was "crippled". My destiny and purpose were handicapped by my own doing. I could not help myself. It was an endless and burdensome struggle until God's Truth told me, *"Come as you are and Gather around the Father's love."*

The Father called my name and sent people to look for me; He took me from my land of nothingness and brokenness. I chose to check myself into the "Father's Love Rehab Center." Although not a physical building, this was a new season I entered, giving the Father full permission to cleanse, heal, renew and deliver me.

When I checked into God's Word, there He washed the filth out of my mind, and expelled the tormenting demons that had me imprisoned. After having discovered the Father's love, I chose to move in- to move in permanently with Him. I never wanted to submit to the tormenting thoughts, the fear, and the lies from the enemy, ever again.

WHAT DO YOU DO WHEN THE MOST IMPORTANT PERSON IN HEAVEN AND EARTH HAS CHOSEN YOU?

- You choose to spend the rest of your life exploring the Love of the Father.
- You choose to surrender to God's Word and God's Love.
- You choose to have Him as your Father, your Commander, your captain, your EVERYTHING!
- You choose to let Him have His way, do it His way, and use His healing methods. (My ways had not worked for me anyway, and the pain of my defeat was making me even more helpless.)

SO, DO YOU WANT TO GET WELL?

I greatly enjoy the story of John 5:6:

"When Jesus saw him lying and learned that he had been in this condition for a long time, he asked him, 'do you want to get well?'. 'Sir', the invalid replied, 'I have no one to help me into the pool when the water is stirred. While I am trying to get in, someone else goes down ahead of me.' Then Jesus said to him, 'Get up! Pick up your mat and walk.'"

INVALID

- Invalid is a term used for something that is *not* legally or officially acceptable.
- Invalid is a person with chronic illness, weakness.
- Invalidate means to remove someone from active service.

The Spirit of Rejection has one goal, which is to remove you from active service. The Spirit of Rejection works through fear to remove you from active service to the heavenly Father, active service to your family and active service to your purpose and destiny.

The Spirit of Rejection will keep its captives lying down in the same place for a long time with no progress, no advancement, in a position of defeat, and it will make you helpless.

The invalid in the story had no one to help, no one to push him. He had no one; not even himself. He had accepted his condition and mentally checked out.

The first push must come from inside of you, by your spirit man.

The invalid was so used to being cast aside, ignored, too late, etc. He had "almost-there" syndrome. But when Jesus came as the Godsend to help him, he did not know that the hour of his visitation had come. He was stuck with the reality of his past circumstances, and ignoring the reality of the Most Important Person, Jesus, talking to him.

REFLECTIONS

1. What have you accepted and mentally "checked out" of?
2. Where are you stuck with the reality of your past circumstances, and ignoring the reality of Jesus Christ talking to you?

CHAPTER 12

The Spirit of Rejection usually takes advantage of any kind of trauma, abandonment or rejection. It attacks those most vulnerable, and usually comes during the early years of life. Children are the most vulnerable because they look up to their parents to shape their worth, world, identity, and purpose. And parents are constantly painting pictures of the Heavenly Father's love to young children. What an awesome responsibility!

Children believe what they see more than what they are told. Children define normal based on what they experience regularly. Mephibosheth was just 5 years old when his whole world changed. His father and grandfather, who were the most influential men in Israel at the time, were running for their lives, which could not understand. He thought, "Daddy was this powerful man, and everybody listened to him. What happened? What is going on? Can someone talk to me?" Children understand a lot more than what adults give them credit for.

It's said that a child's worth is shaped between the ages of 0-12 years. It is not coincidental that my trouble with rejection started on my 5th birthday.

Jesus was so loved by his parents that at the age of 12, he was confident enough to stand among adults asking questions and teaching the word. (Luke 2:42 NIV)

Children are full of faith, and they are born with God-like abilities, believing they can change the world and even fix their parents' problems, until an adult or other influence talks them out of these great imaginations through unbelief, fear and neglect.

Children are also full of needs; love needs. They are like sponges soaking in anything you give them. That is why the father asked us to approach the kingdom of God like a child. When their love needs are not met in childhood, they are predisposed to being hurt even more, being taken advantage of, and/or hurting other people.

REFLECTIONS

What are those events that happened to you at age 0-12 that:

1. painted a positive picture of the Father's love?
2. painted a negative picture of the Father's love?

IT IS NOT YOUR FAULT

Mephibosheth was crippled in both feet, but it was not his own fault. His nurse was running to save his life from those who sought to kill the king's son, and she was trying to escape with him when he fell and became crippled. Things could have been worse; thank God he did not die from the fall or become brain dead.

Thank God you did not die from what happened to you! Thank God you are alive to tell the story and change the story.

It was not his fault that he fell. *He* had not done anything evil to anyone. Evil was pursuing *him*, and evil was happening *to* him.

The Spirit of Rejection works with the Spirit of False Accusation which sounds like:

- "It is your fault that the accident took place."
- "It is your fault that the person died."
- "It is your fault that your parents got a divorce."
- "It is your fault that you were sexually violated or exploited."
- "It is your fault that no one loves you."
- "It is your fault that you are all alone."

It is the Spirit of *False* Accusation because nothing that is being said aligns with the truth of God's Word and the truth of the Father's Love. The heavenly Father does not accuse you. Even when you are wrong, He acquits you and advocates for you with His love and His righteousness.

As the scriptures say,

"Therefore, no condemnation now exists for those in Christ Jesus."
(Romans 8:1 NIV)

*"Who is there to condemn us? For Christ Jesus who died, and more than that was raised to life, is at the right hand of God. and **He is interceding for us.**"*

(Romans 8:34 NIV)

Condemnation means very strong disapproval; it is the act of punishing or sentencing someone. When you accept the devil's lie that it is your fault, the trauma of your childhood continues and follows you into adulthood. The strong disapproval you give yourself becomes a prison and a sentence to your destiny and purpose.

You may continue to exist, but you are dismissed from service, made *invalid* and no longer useful because of the sentence of disapproval that you gave yourself.

"His disciples asked him, 'Rabbi who sinned, this man or his parents, that he was born blind?' 'Neither this man nor his parents sinned,' said Jesus, 'but it happened so that the works of God might be displayed in Him. It happened so that the power of God could be seen in him'"

(John 9:2 NIV)

Human beings are constantly looking for who is responsible and who will take the blame or the guilt. The disciples were trying to ascribe guilt and punishment. "Is it the man himself who sinned?"

Have people blamed you for the trouble that has happened to you? Have you blamed your parents for the trouble that you are going through? Your parents may well be wrong, but they also have their parents to blame for their own actions, and the chain continues until we all blame Adam and Eve.

Jesus, however, *was* not and *is* not interested in who caused the problem; he is interested in who is ready to get well! *"Do you want to be healed?"* He asked the invalid man. Instead of blaming your parents who abandoned you, your ex who betrayed you, your government who disfavored you, and Mr. Nobody who always follows you and never helps you, today, Jesus is saying to you, "Let me show you my power. The power of my love to rescue you and take away your blindness.

I am here. I am the Father you never had. The Help you never received. The Love you always longed for. Stop the excuses and pick up the mat you have been lying down on."

- the mat of your past
- the mat of the life you never had
- the mat of discrimination
- the mat of the abuse and neglect
- the mat of all your weaknesses and disadvantages
- the mat of your rejection and fears

RISE UP AND WALK

Jesus is saying "stop the description of your problem, your pain, your shame, your loss". Let me start with the elaborate description of Mr. Answer, Your Help, Your Solution; The Heavenly Father. Jesus did not ask the invalid man what happened to him and how long he was invalid …Jesus only asked if he wanted to be well!

DO YOU WANT TO BE WELL?

Do you want to give up the control and attention that your pain and brokenness have earned you so far? Many people receive disability advantages, but they care nothing about being free or being made whole.

> *"Many people receive disability advantages, but they care nothing about being free or being made whole."*

I remember the story of a lame beggar in a wheelchair where an Evangelist asked if he could pray for him. He said, "please pray that God will bless me today with many people to put money in my beggar's basket." The evangelist told him, "Jesus has much more to offer; Jesus wants to make you walk!" The beggar said, "Oh no! I am the President of the Lame People's Association. It took me years to earn that title."

Can you imagine? While you might think how crazy someone would be to pass up the healing touch of Jesus Christ, it happens more often than you would think. Again, Jesus asked you if you want to be well because He *can*, and He *wants* to make you whole. He is the only one who can make you whole.

JESUS TOOK THE BLAME

Jesus said,

"Father forgive them for they do not know what they are doing."

(Luke 23:34 NIV)

> *"Jesus said let me not only make you whole; let me make sure this never happens to you again. He made you whole so that you will never attract brokenness or broken people again."*

So, whose fault is it? Jesus answered that question on the cross when he told the Heavenly Father to forgive you, for you do not know what you are doing. Jesus also asked that the Father forgive all those who hurt you for they do not know what they are doing. Jesus took the blame for your sin. He took the blame for your parents' sin, He took the blame for your ex's sin and *all* those who took advantage of you.

Jesus said let me not only make you whole; let me make sure this never happens to you again. He made you whole so that you will never attract brokenness or broken people again. He is a good God! Praise His wonderful Name.

BLAME AND SHAME

Blame and shame go hand in hand. The one who bears the blame carries shame; And the one who gives out blame gives out shame. You cannot give what you do not have. If you are giving out blame, it is because you have much of it inside of you. If you are giving out shame, there is a lot of hidden shame inside of you. But there is good news for you! Jesus came as your burden bearer, your shame bearer, and your blame bearer.

"But in fact, He has borne our griefs, And He has carried our sorrows and pains…

But he was wounded for our transgressions; he was crushed for our wickedness (our sin, our injustice, our wrongdoing)

The punishment required for our wellbeing fell on Him. And by his stripes (wounds), we are healed."

(Isaiah 53:3 AMP)

REFLECTIONS

---

1. What shame am I carrying?
2. What burdens have made one with me?

CHAPTER 13

The Spirit of Rejection is an oppressive spirit that causes people to feel unwanted, unloved and not useful. It usually comes from abandonment and childhood trauma, but it can also come in through betrayal, losses, and disappointments in adulthood. The Spirit of Rejection comes in through a lie that a person believes. It can also cause ungodly attachments and entanglements that make no room for attachments to God. This is the beginning of idolatry.

The Spirit of Rejection makes people feel there is nobody to help:

NOBODY TO HELP YOU AT BIRTH

- born out of wedlock
- unwanted child
- difficult pregnancy or delivery (mentally, emotionally)

- parents divorced or separated in early childhood
- alcoholic or drug abusing parents
- unknown biological father or mother
- presence of mother that was abused or is suffering from the Spirit of Rejection

NOBODY TO HELP IN CHILDHOOD

- "only child syndrome" (no one to play with)
- "first child syndrome" (all the responsibility on you)
- "middle child syndrome" (lost in the crowd)
- "last child syndrome" (have to meet up to parents' and siblings' expectations)
- abandonment (financial crises, divorce, sickness, death, job and relocations)

NOBODY TO HELP IN TEENAGE YEARS

- misunderstood by parents and siblings
- misunderstood by classmates (bullied, made fun of, left out)
- misused by predators (sexual exploitation, other socially delinquent activities)
- mishaps (unwanted pregnancy, unwanted marriage and commitments, school dropout etc.)

Most of the above scenarios would not have happened if you had someone to help. Someone to talk to, someone to listen, someone to guide or instruct you.

> *"Where there is no counsel, the people fall; But in the multitude of counselors, there is safety.*
>
> *Where there is no governor, the people shall fall; but there is safety where there is much counsel."*
>
> **(Proverbs 11:14 NIV)**

Children raised without a governor, a guide, and no loving boundaries are usually ensnared into the miserable hands of the Spirit of Rejection.

IN SEARCH OF SOMEONE TO HOLD

Every child is born with the desire to be loved, held close, fed, and receive the loving caregiver's attention.

The four main needs of man are:

- acceptance (sense of belonging)
- identity (sense of uniqueness)
- security (sense of safety)
- purpose (sense of usefulness)

> *"Start children off on the way they should go, and even when they are old, they will not turn from it."*
>
> **(Proverb 22:6 NIV)**

These needs can only be truly met by God, and God gave parents the awesome privilege of raising children. He also gave parents the ability to point the children to the Loving Father, who will meet these inner needs. When parents draw the child to God's love, the child's inner needs are met. The behaviors of parents shape the foundation of their children.

Parents are to:

- turn towards the Heavenly Father, the source of all Love and goodness
- turn towards one another (father and mother)
- turn towards the child and the siblings by loving impartially and making every child feel special
- Turn towards your destiny and future (the example that parents set forth shapes the child's future)

But when the parent draws the child to their own brokenness and away from God, these needs remain unmet.

Parents can create insecurities in their children through:

- perfectionism: when the child believes his performance is more important to the parent than himself.
- possessiveness: "I have only you; I cannot lose you; my world will fall apart." The child carries the blame for the parent's dysfunction.
- passivity: the child hears that *"you are not worth the investment."*
- controlling: parent(s) do(es) not give the child the freedom to grow, or the trust that the child needs, to succeed.

- drug abusive parents: the parents are addicted to alcohol and drugs, and therefore unable to care for a child.
- abusive parents: the child hears, *"You are nothing, you deserve nothing, you will amount to nothing, I want others to treat you this way…"*

When children grow up without seeds of love planted in them, they have neediness, discontentment and lack of worth that attracts the companionship of the Spirit of Rejection and the Spirit of Fear. These spirits work hand in hand and keep company any heart that is crushed and feeling worthless, abandoned or insecure.

CHAPTER 14

Forgiveness is the first gift the Father gives you. Forgiveness is the first gift the Father expects you to give those who hurt you. It is an act of your will in obedience to the Father, and a response to the forgiveness we have received from God. Forgiveness is the act of choosing to continue to receive God's forgiveness. Forgiveness is the notice of release you serve to your tormentors and prisoner wardens.

"If you forgive those who sin against you, your heavenly Father will forgive you. But if your refuse to forgive others, your Father will not forgive your sins."

(Matthew 6:14 NIV)

Name those who sinned against you and forgive them. You will be releasing yourself from the trap of waiting for them to be served justice. Leave that to God; he says vengeance is mine.

FORGIVE

- your father
- your mother
- your brothers and sisters
- that cousin, uncle, aunt
- that boyfriend or girlfriend
- your husband
- your wife
- your in-laws
- those who betrayed you, belittled you, blamed you, bashed you, bartered you, beat you down, broke your heart, dreams, and expectations.

FORGIVE AND LET GO

Now forgive yourself. Let yourself go from your own prison walls of expectations and the questions of blame asking, "How could I have?"

Start by asking God to forgive you for:

- running and hiding
- despising your birthright like Esau
- comparing yourself with others
- trying to be who you are not
- putting the opinion of men above that of God
- holding on to the hurt and the pain

Now receive the Father's forgiveness! His forgiveness is His welcome home! It is the Father saying, *"come close."* It is His "second chance" offering to you. **Do not turn down his love and mercy. Receive his forgiveness and let yourself go.**

> *"If we confess our sins, he is faithful and just and will forgive us our sins and purify us from all unrighteousness."*

(1 John 1:9 NIV)

> *"Now start watering the seed of forgiveness that the Father has put in your heart by turning the page of your past."*

(Philippians 3:13 NIV)

And remember, my dear brothers and sisters, forget the past and look forward to what lies ahead.

CHAPTER 15

DESTROYING THE MAN-MADE STRONGHOLDS

Jesus came to set the captives free! This is my story and my reality. My testimony of deliverance is a testimony of the Grace of God that delivers and transforms. My whole personality, disposition, desires and ambitions were changed by a touch of the Father's Love.

In 2008, when my wonderful husband began to teach and minister in church on a deliverance series, I was kind of surprised about his choice of theme for such a well-behaved audience. I actually became a little upset that the teaching went on and on for many weeks. I asked him one Sunday why he was so passionate about deliverance, and if there were no other interesting sermons he could pick from. He answered me, saying, "but that is what Jesus came to do; He came to set the captives free."

At the time, I had the false belief that people tormented by evil spirits would only be found only in a mental institution or a prison cell. I never thought that functional people like myself could be demonized.

The pastor asked all the church members to read the book *They Shall Expel Demons* by Derek Prince; one of the books we now highly recommend for deliverance. After resisting for a while, I decided to read just to fulfill my duties, particularly since I did not want to be put on the spot or asked questions about the book having not engaged in the reading.

Now I know that it was absolutely demonic activity influencing me to resist the teaching on deliverance and causing me to think that it was not for me. When I finally began to read the book, I saw my own story, a mirror of my life. Derek Prince explained how rejection and emotional shock could open the door to many demons, including spirits of infirmities and allergies. I was so shocked as I had suffered in childhood with many visits to the doctor, unexplained and untreatable skin diseases, I also had many allergies, and I was prone to accidents, injury and falls.

Soon, I began to desire to be free from the things that I had accepted as part of me, such as:

- extreme shyness and social phobias
- loneliness and difficulty making friends
- fear of rejection, self-pity, and complaining
- forgetfulness, mediocrity, and laziness
- mood swings
- pride, self-justification, excuses, resistance to correction
- self-neglect, hatred for taking pictures, or no satisfaction with pictures, hatred of my voice, and love of black colored things
- critical spirit, judgmental, and religious spirits

- allergies
- fear of man, fear of darkness, fear of flying and creeping insects.

My husband began to minister to me and commanded that the spirit come out in the name of Jesus. And one after the other, they left my body. Some of them left with no manifestations, and others came out screaming. By the time we finished the sessions of ministry, I felt like a new person. I felt lighter, brighter and cleaner. That was the beginning of a whole new ministry for my husband, myself and our church. Even my family members could tell something supernatural had taken place.

As I told my testimony to my mom, the light of God was exposing her own struggles, and she shared with me part of her childhood that I had no idea about before then. My mom had struggled with the Spirit of Rejection, as well. She was one of 5 children, but when she was about 5 years old, she was taken away from her parents to live with a family friend, a couple who were not able to have children of their own. It is no coincidence that my feelings of abandonment and torment occurred at 5-years old as well.

This is a common tradition in some parts of Africa, where the whole community shares the responsibility of raising the children. Couples who have too many children can willingly give one child or two to a couple who have no children, to raise them- like foster parents. My mom only got to know her parents and siblings later in her life. The feeling of abandonment made her think and ask the "*why me*" question. "*Of all my siblings, why was I the one given away at such a young age? Did my parents prefer the other children to me? Do I really belong to my biological family or to the family that raised me?"* These questions make it hard for a child to feel like they fit in and have a sense of belonging and acceptance. This emotional trauma created a wound of rejection, self-pity and self-doubt.

My Mom also told me the emotional challenges she experienced when she was pregnant with me. I believe that all these incidents contributed to opening the door to the Spirit of Rejection in me at such a young age, even though I grew up in a loving family and a very God-fearing and warm environment.

THE WOMB

The womb is an atmosphere that sets the baby up to be either a *victor* or a *victim*. The fetus is alive and able to hear the words spoken around it while in the womb. John the Baptist was filled with the Holy Spirit from within the womb. He *leaped* in the womb to give glory to Jesus, who was still in Mary's womb at the time. Both babies were already communicating with each other.

Let no one fool you that babies are not alive in the womb; they have a well-developed heart at just six weeks. Getting rid of the fetus in the womb is committing murder.

REFLECTIONS

It is important to:

1. know what happened concerning your birth
2. know what the circumstances were concerning your conception
3. know what the circumstances were concerning your mother's pregnancy
4. know whether your parents were rejoicing at your birth
5. let the light of God shine in every hidden corner and uncover every darkness

CHAPTER 16

"When an evil spirit leaves a person, it goes into the desert, seeking a resting place, but finding none, it says, 'I will return to the person I came from.' So, it returns and finds its former home empty, swept and clean. Then the spirit finds seven other spirits, more evil than itself, and they all enter the person and live there. And the person is worse off than before."

(Matthew 12:43 NIV)

From the beginning of our journey, we met the Father's love that transfers us from the Land of Brokenness, Bondage, Slavery, and Scarcity to the Land of Completeness and Wholeness.

We saw how Mephibosheth changed addresses from Lo-Debar to live in Jerusalem with King David. When God is ready to do something great in your life, He will change your address too. The evil spirits said, "we will return to our home," in the person who was already set free. Demonic spirits roam around looking for a home that will receive them.

In deliverance, we compel demons to give up their hold on us. Your body, your mind, your emotions *were* their home. Demons cannot live in the *spirit* of a believer since the Holy Spirit dwells in our spirit. But they can *infect* and *infiltrate* the unrenewed mind of the believer, creating a nest and strongholds from where they influence and manipulate your thoughts and actions.

In deliverance, you serve the demonic spirits with an eviction notice. Demons are rebellious, just like their master the devil, and will not go until *you* force them out. Deliverance is the process of throwing them out with *all* their belongings.

You need to get to a place where you are angry enough with what the enemy has stolen from you and your family that you *violently* kick him out of your life.

"But you have saved us from our adversaries, and you have put to shame those who hate us."

(Psalm 44:7 NIV)

The Spirit of Rejection and the Spirit of Fear are your enemies; they hate you and hate your identity in God. They will do everything possible, finding seven more wicked spirits to join them in their efforts to torment, oppress and limit you. It is time to push them out and throw out *all* their belongings.

SOME OF THE BELONGINGS OF THE SPIRIT OF REJECTION:

Broken and dysfunctional relationships	Codependence	Independence	Ingratitude
Rebellion and arrogance	Mediocrity	Perfectionism	Chronic illness
Hypocrisy	Accidents and being accident-prone	Fear of man, people pleasing	Double mindedness and confusion
Excess talkativeness, lying, exaggerations	Excess appetite (for sex, for food, drugs, alcohol)	Excess emotions (anger, rage, hypersensitivity, jealousy)	Excess confidence (boasting, bashing,
Excess attachments to things, people, time, positions, goals, work.	Excess loneliness (depression, suicide)	Excess rest (laziness, procrastination, excuses)	Excessive work (misplaced priorities)
[Need for control]			

Above a few of the manifestations that appear along with the Spirit of Rejection.

I made a list of all these, renouncing them one after the other and separating my spirit, soul and body from their influences. I reject each and every one of their gifts and offers. Then we took authority over the demons and casted them out in the name of Jesus.

"In my name, they shall cast out demons…"

(Mark 16:16 NIX)

> *That is why you need to change your address so that when your enemy (Spirit of Rejection and Fear) returns to your street, he cannot recognize your house.*

I encourage you to make your own list and do the same. The bible says when the demons leave, they go to the desert. Demons like dry, arid places. They hang around you when you are dry, cold, and empty. The Lord Jesus has disarmed the devil, so he roams around, taking advantage of the weak, the broken, the desperate and the lonely. That is why you need to change your address so that when your enemy (Spirit of Rejection and Fear) returns to your street, he cannot recognize your house. They will pass you by without noticing you because you are not the same person. Their home in you will have been demolished, and you have put up a brand-new structure with new thoughts, new imaginations, new words and new actions. A home under new management.

THINGS TO DEMOLISH AND THINGS TO DEVELOP

"The weapons we fight with are not the weapons of the world. On the contrary, they have divine power to demolish strongholds. We demolish arguments and every pretension that sets itself up against the knowledge of God, and we take captive every thought to make it obedient to Christ."

(2 Corinthians 10:4-5 NIV)

We can demolish every deceptive fantasy that opposes God and break through every arrogant attitude raised up in defiance of the true knowledge of God. Like prisoners of war, we capture every thought and insist that it bow in obedience to the Anointed One.

Casting out demonic spirits is only the beginning of the war. Actually, after your deliverance, the enemy comes after you *more violently*. However, that should not be a reason for you not to seek your deliverance. No! After deliverance, you release the power of God that is in you, and much more effective against the enemy. The battles may be more, but they will become much easier to win and overcome. Hallelujah!

After my deliverance, I did not instantly become bold, outgoing and joyful. These are new structures that the Holy Spirit put up in my mind and personality as I spent time feasting at the Father's table of love. However, the paralyzing fear that I used to experience when in front of people was gone. The constant oppressive thoughts of "not good enough" had broken their influence over my mind.

I was freed from the misery of trying to be perfect and forcing others to be perfect. I could accept my imperfection and make room for the imperfections of others. I gave myself the room and the patience to grow, to make mistakes and to learn.

Cast out the evil spirits and cut down their systems of operation by:

- dismantling the defenses behind which the Spirit of Rejection has been hidden
- demolishing every deceptive fantasy about yourself, people or circumstances

- breaking every arrogant attitude
- opposing every idea or feeling that prevents you from experiencing the Father's love
- capturing like a prisoner every thought that rebels against the love of the Father
- insisting that your thoughts bow in obedience to Jesus Christ

CHAPTER 17

*"So, get rid of your old self, which made you live as used to-the old self
that has been destroyed by its deceitful desires."*

(Ephesians 4:22 NIV)

Your old self includes your old ways of thinking about the Father's love. Your old self was destroyed by deception. The deceitful imaginations that you had about the Father being a distant, unevolved and demanding father. These old and deceptive thoughts birthed the old/natural you that felt worthless, unattractive, not useful, and unloved. The old self had built strongholds of rejection, disfavor, limitation and imitation. It is time for all the towers of deception and blindness to come down. Amen.

ARISE AND SHINE

"Arise and shine, for your light has come."

(Isaiah 60:1 NIV)

The Lord Jesus told the invalid man to arise and go home. Pick up your mat, arise from a low perspective of God. You will be able to see yourself clearer and better when you see yourself through the Father's loving eyes.

In 2015, on one of our missions' trips to South Africa, I had a night vision in which the Holy Spirt came asking me about the name of our women's ministry- Arise and Shine Women's Ministry. He asked me, *"What are you calling the women to arise from?"*. I was taken aback, as I had never thought about that before. Then all of a sudden, I saw in a vision handwriting on the wall, spelling the word ARISE vertically, with each letter spelling out the attitude that the women were to arise from.

This was what Holy Spirit wants His women to arise from;

- **A**RROGANCE
- **R**EJECTION
- **I**NGRATITUDE
- **S**ELFISH AMBITION
- **E**XCUSES

I was amazed, and this began the journey of uprooting these strongholds and building new towers of Love.

> *Excuses stem from the ignorance of not knowing how useful you are to the Father and his purposes on earth.*

Arrogance stems from the ignorance of the Father as the Source of All Good Things. All our accomplishments come from him. Without God, we are nothing and can do nothing. Arrogance is misplaced identity. Rejection stems from the ignorance of The Father as a Lover and Defender. Rejections lead to insecurities.

Ingratitude limits your capacity to experience the abundant Love of the Father because gratitude is the seed for increase. Selfish Ambition stems from the ignorance of the abundance that the Father has given to you for others. Excuses stem from the ignorance of not knowing how useful you are to the Father and his purposes on earth.

CHAPTER 18

"I am doing a brand-new thing, something unheard of. Even now, it sprouts and grows and matures. Don't you perceive it? I will make a way in the wilderness and open up flowing streams in the desert. Wild beasts, jackals and owls will glorify me. For I will supply streams of water in the desert and rivers in the wilderness to satisfy the thirst of my people, my chosen ones, so that you, whom I have shaped and formed for myself, will proclaim my praise."

(Isaiah 43:19-21 NIV)

The Father is doing a new thing; He is putting up a brand new structure in you!

The 3 stages that of the new building are:

- Sprouting
- Growing
- Maturing

The Father wants you to perceive it, to see it, to behold what he is doing! He wants you to have a preview of His new production. The Father is opening flowing streams. The rivers of life will satisfy your every longing. Like the Samaritan woman, you will not have to go back to carry water from the well or rely on the affection and attention of men for validation and significance. The Father's Love will become a fountain of life flowing inside of you. The dry places in your life, dry emotions, dry feelings, dry relationships, and lacking intimacy with the Father are all going to be flooded with the Light of the Father's Love.

Are you ready for the move?

"Everyone who loves is fathered by God and experiences intimate knowledge of him."

(1 John 4:7 NIV)

"May you experience the love of Christ, though it is so great to understand fully. Then you will be made complete with all the fullness of life and power that comes from God."

(Ephesians 3:19 NIV)

The land of completeness and wholeness is *experiencing the Father's love.*

~PRAYER~

Heavenly Father, I have known you as my God, but today I accept and receive you as my Abba Father. Grant me an experience of your love. Grant me to become rooted and grounded in your love. Grant me a continuous awareness of the place I have in your heart.

Thank you, Heavenly Father, that Your love is molding and shaping out of me a brand-new person who receives love and gives love with the same intensity that the Heavenly Father poured into me. Amen!

The Good Father has just responded to your prayer and wants you to know what he thinks about you.

"I WANT YOU, MY CHILD"

*"His people will be called the holy people, the saved People of the Lord, and Jerusalem will be called **the city God wants, the city God has not rejected**."*

(Isaiah 62:12 NIV)

The Father has changed your name, just as he changed the name of Jacob (Supplanter) to Israel (Prince of God). He is giving you a new name. He called you **the city that God wants,** and you can adopt that new name and new title.

No longer will you be called:

- The Rejected City

- The Abandoned city

- The Forgotten City

- The Barren City

- The Lonely City

- The Bleeding City

- The Slave City

- The Filthy City

- The Unattractive City

- The Depressed City

Take some time and accept your permanent exile from your desert land (or whatever name/circumstance used to manifest in your life). Now write down your new name; the Father calls you! The "Sought-out Child."; "My favorite child".

There is something so special about children that are sought after. They have so much value to the parent, more than the children that come easy.

The Father says you are a hard-to-get child. He paid for your adoption with the life of His Only Begotten Son; you are not just anybody; you are special to Him.

Pause and give Abba Father some praise

REFLECTIONS

Take some time and accept your permanent exile from your desert land, (or whatever name/circumstance used to manifest in your life).

Now write down your new name that the Father called you:

_____

THE FATHER *WANTS* ME

WANTS ME

ACCEPTS ME

NEEDS ME

TRUSTS ME

SURROUNDS ME

Say these statements over and over again to yourself until every fiber of your being believes it and begins to explode with the love of God.

When I received the revelation that the Father wants me, it changed everything about how I treated myself. Holiness and righteousness were no longer a duty or just some laws to follow; it became a code of conduct because my value had changed. The value of my life has been greatly appreciated by the One who wants me. Like the price of a car in an auction depends on the highest bidder, God gave the highest price to own you, and he set a new price and value over your life.

There is a desire in every heart to be wanted, to be celebrated to be desired and special to someone significant. The Most Important Person of the earth says He wants you.

Abba Father accepts you, (Ephesians 1:6). He accepts you and sees all your strengths and weaknesses. All your shortcomings and flaws. He accepts you unconditionally. In spite of you, he accepts you because you are His beloved child.

The Father trusts you. He trusted you with His very life. He placed the Holy Spirit inside of you. He is the treasure of heaven in earthen vessels. So, the Father has His life investments deposited in you. You are God's glorious inheritance in the saints (Ephesians1:18).

TRUTHS

• The Father trusts me, calms all my fears and blows my insecurities away. (I always wanted to be more and do more, but I am now liberated to be myself, dream big and be extraordinary, just meditating on the fact that the Father trusts me).

- He trusts that I can be more and do more
- He trusts me to do greater things than these
- He trusts that I will never leave him nor forsake him
- He trusts that I will run the race to the end and overcome
- He trusts me by revealing His secrets to me, sharing His plans with me

This kind of love just makes it easier for you to trust God even more and give him even more of yourself.

HE FATHER SURROUNDS ME

"Let your unfailing love surround us, Lord, for our hope is in You alone."

(Psalm 33:22 NIV)

The word surround means to "enclose on all sides". To surround also means to enclose like a body of troops so as to cut off communication. The love of God is so wide and long. His love is so high and deep. The Father's love encloses you and your whole destiny on all sides. His love is a body of troops that cuts off all communications with the Spirit of Rejection and the Spirit of Fear. The love of God casts away every fear...You are never alone. His love *always* surrounds you.

One thing that the Father does that brings me such joy each time I think about it is the fact that the Father actually *surrounds* us, *rejoicing* over us with singing.

You'd better join his choir now! Rejoice in Him, Rejoice *with* Him.

> *"For the Lord your God is living among you. He is a mighty savior. He will take delight in you with gladness."*
>
> *(Zephaniah 3:17 NIV)*

With His love, He will calm all your fears. He will rejoice over you with joyful songs.

CHAPTER 19

"Go to the village ahead of you, and as you enter it, you will find a young donkey tied there, which no one has ever ridden. Untie it and bring it here

If anyone asks, why are you untying that colt? Just say, 'The Lord needs it.'"

(Luke 19:30-31 NIV)

"Father, I want those whom you have given me to be with me where I am. Then they can see all the glory you gave me because you loved me even before the world began."

(John 17:24 NIV)

After my deliverance, I saw beauty through the eyes of the beholder, my Father. He said I was beautiful, and this is what I saw:

B – Beautiful, Beloved

E – Enjoyed

A – Accepted

U – Useful

T – Trained

I – Intimate

F – Faithful

U – Unique

L – Loved

His beloved child who is enjoying:

- the acceptance of the Father.
- being useful to the Father.
- the training from the Father.
- intimacy with the Father.
- being faithful to the Father.
- being loved by the Father.
- being unique to the Father

This is the true definition of beautiful, unfading beauty.

FRUITS OF DELIVERANCE

"But the fruits of the Spirit is love, joy, peace, patience, kindness, goodness, gentleness, faithfulness and self-control."

(Galatians 5:22 NIV)

The demonic influences that empowered the works of the flesh in my life were broken. The Spirit of God had room to work His new life in me.

LOVE

I received freedom to love. I was freed to display my passionate love for my Father. Before my deliverance, I was very self-conscious during worship; I was so people-conscious and would reserve my intense display of love for the Father only for private time of prayer. I remember being so upset with people dancing out of their worship bubble, shouting out during service and being overly expressive. I used to think they were just trying to pull attention to themselves. Do you see how the devil will twist things around? But guess what? As the Holy Spirit would have it, I became that very person! The passionate and disorganized worshipper. I couldn't hold my tears, couldn't contain my joy, and I would dance as if it was just Him and me in the hall, totally oblivious to the crowd. I was freed to love the Father passionately! He permitted me to lose myself in my pursuit to gain all of Him.

I was freed to love people and express my love for them publicly too! I was liberated to thank God for my husband, my children and all my loved ones without thinking of others who do not have what I had. I was freed to receive love. My husband's praises and compliments were no longer offensive to me. I began to enjoy him calling me "the most beautiful woman in the world", and I thought to myself, "If I can receive this, there are no human words that can adequately describe what Abba Father thinks of me, so I can take these words and be grateful to the Father for each one of them."

The Father also showed me that all love comes from Him. Any love, compliment, attention, and kindness I receive from men is actually His hand supplying all my needs.

JOY

Joy was the special kiss that the Father gave me with my welcome home. I received joy as I studied the word of God and how much the Father loves me. I would dance all by myself because the Bible had become a living book to me. From the sad girl who saw no reason to be happy and upset with my husband for always being so happy, I became the one who walks around infecting people with joy. The Father had stripped me of the garments of mourning and given me garments of joy and praise. I am forever grateful.

PEACE

I remember going through a Bible study where I learned that Peace is not the absence of trouble but the presence of the Prince of Peace. The Father moved into my heart and demolished the old building of rejection. He put up His new residence of Love, and the flag that He placed on my porch as a sign of His new government was peace. I received from the Father the ability to stay calm even as things come out of order.

Before my deliverance, I used to get so agitated, distracted, and anxious when things were not going according to plan. I would pass notes to my husband, kick his leg under the table and used many other manipulative words and attitudes to ensure that things go right according to me. Well, it never really worked. Things and people still failed me constantly. I also failed myself. So, I took up the Father's offer; *"…and in all things, give thanks for this is the will of God in Christ Jesus concerning you"* (1 Thessalonians 5:18 NKJV). Thanking God when things are *not* working is far from being easy, yet it is the *easiest* way to restore your peace, for in thanksgiving you acknowledge the presence of the Prince of Peace, and you get plugged into his River of Peace. The Father gave me peace with God and peace with *myself.*

His love ceased the war of self-rejection. He stilled the storms of self-defense and quieted the noise of craving for the attention and approval of people. The Father gave me peace with my assignment.

His love helped me stop running away from the call to ministry, to be a pastor, a preacher, and a mother in Israel. I rejected the call because I didn't see myself fit to stand before people. The paralysis of "fear of man" led me to reject that I was an intercessor, thus I had a backgrounded and hidden ministry. I was hiding; I was afraid and tormented by the Spirit of Fear. The Father gave me peace with *who* I am and *whose* I am. He gave me peace about my calling.

He gave me peace about being different and peace about standing out. He told me once, "Elizabeth, you praise Me as the Awesome God, there is no one like me, and say I stand out in my own class. How can you be my child and stand beside Me as My bride and expect not to stand out?" That was eye-opening and mind-blowing. His Love liberated me to run my race, not comparing myself with others. His acceptance licensed me to stay in my lane and be exceptional and stop giving excuses for mediocrity. The Father's love permitted me to shine, to be distinguished, and to be beautiful!

NEW ATTIRE

I changed my closet completely after my deliverance. I went from having all-black shoes and navy-blue outfits to every color of the rainbow in my closet. The Father caused me to look at the flowers and said: "Look how I dress the lilies; they all stand out and beautify your surroundings." He said, "I want to dress you up, my daughter from inside out; you will beautify my surroundings with your love."

PATIENCE

Having received peace with the Father and applying that peace to myself, it was easier to live in peace and harmony with all men. I was delivered from finding fault, being critical and judgmental. The Father's love put patience with people into my heart, and I made room for their mistakes and room for others, including myself, to grow. Kindness and gentleness also came along with His love.

SELF-CONTROL

Self-Control is losing your right to control a situation, people or an outcome. This was a fruit that took some time for me to understand. The Spirit of Rejection has its own way of controlling a person that could appear to be self-controlled. And because I was very quiet, withdrawn and passive, I could easily be mistaken for a humble, obedient and self-controlled person.

Self-Control, which is the fruit of the Spirit, means to come under the control of another Person -The Holy Spirit. It means driving under the influence of the Holy Spirit. The Spirit of Fear and Rejection wants your flesh to be in control. It wants you to avoid pain by defending yourself or hurting them before they hurt you, always being in control.

The Father invites you to surrender your control (your understanding, protection, and backup systems) to His love. He wants you to fully trust Him to take care of you and be in control. It is receiving the Father's control and accepting His right as owner over you, your life and your circumstances.

If you lose your *right*, then you gain His *right hand*. If you hold onto your right, then you lose His right hand.

CHAPTER 20

HE'S LOOKING FOR YOU

"Go to the village ahead of you, and as you enter it, you will find a young donkey tied there, which no one has ever ridden. Untie it and bring it here. If anyone asks, why are you untying that colt? Just say 'The Lord needs it'"

(Luke 19:30-31 NIV)

"Father, I want these whom you have given me to be with me where I am. Then they can see all the glory you gave me because you loved me even before the world began."

(John 17:24 NIV)

The Love of the Father will leave the ninety-nine sheep to come after the:

- one lost
- one broken
- one abandoned
- one hurting
- one handicapped
- one weary
- one afraid
- one unworthy
- one rejected

You are that donkey he is looking for. You are the donkey in the village, in hiding, in obscurity, in the crowd, that He has put His eyes on. He wants *you.*

I used to ask myself, "why does God want me?" I accepted that he loved me but had a hard time accepting that he could use me in ministry, especially having received so many prophetic words about what God wants to do in my life and through me. My unworthiness would make me wonder why He would pick such a fearful person. I used to say, "Lord, there are so many more talented, more eloquent, more attractive and more spiritual people than myself; why are you wasting your time with me? See how slow I am to learn and respond to your love?" The Father's amazing love and patience gently answered me, casting away my fears with these words:

> *"Remember, dear brothers and sisters, that few of you were wise in the world's eyes or powerful or wealthy when God called you. Instead, God chose things the world considers foolish in order to shame those who think they are wise."*
>
> *(1 Corinthians 1:26 NIV)*

> *"He chose things that are powerless to shame those who are powerful."*

He uses things that are powerless to shame those who are powerful. Like the donkey, the Master has decreed that you be untied, to be freed, and to be loosed from all your past limitations, your accusations and disqualifications. The Father has already sent word to your previous boss or slave master to, "Let my child go now!" The reason the Father unties you is because He *needs* you. The heavenly Father needs *you*! You are valuable and useful to Him! The donkey was brought to Jesus, and he sat on it and went to the temple where he chased out all the money exchangers and renamed His temple, Isaiah 56:7 "*My house shall be called the house of prayer for all nations*".

My deliverance was the beginning of our deliverance ministry. The Father used my story and my testimony to set others free. I have a special burden for young people who are oppressed with shame and blame, and who are emotionally lame. The Father untied me so that He can use me to untie others; this is what He desires to do with your life. Let him turn your mourning to dancing, and use you to turn other people's mourning into dancing.

The next purpose of your deliverance is so that you may become one with Jesus, and His prayer to the Father may be fulfilled.

- The Father wants you where He is
- The Father wants you doing what He is doing
- The Father wants you to say what He is saying

The Father longs for your company. He longs to have you as a close companion. He longs to hold you and walk with you hand in hand. Yes, He longs to see your face.

"For you are my dove, hidden in the split-open rock.

It was I who took you and hid you up high in the secret stairway of the sky.

Let me see your radiant face and hear your sweet voice.

How beautiful your eyes of worship and lovely your voice in prayer."

(Song of Songs 2:14 NIV)

CARRIED TO THE TABLE OF THE LORD

You have been carried to the table, seated where you now belong. You have been carried to the table swept away by the Father's love. You will never feel your brokenness anymore because the Father hides you in that split-open rock, where He alone can see you, touch you and change you. You will no longer hide within yourself, within your pain, in your own gain, nor in any man-made concerns. The Father is taking you over to hide you in His secret stairway for Himself. Inside the secret place of His love, your face will become radiant with joy unspeakable and full of glory.

As a sheep, you will hear and know the Shepherd's voice. His word will make your voice sweet and strong. Your heart of worship and your voice of prayer will bind your heart and your affections to the heavenly Father. My beloved is mine, and I am His; His banner over me is love.

THE FATHER ENJOYS YOUR COMPANY

I remember one of my business trips in 2017. I was traveling alone this time. My husband and I usually travel together for ministry; we actually do almost everything together. And because of our airline loyalty with Delta airlines, we usually get the privilege of flying first-class.

First-class on an international flight is like being in another world compared to economy class. You are welcomed on board by name, seated at your seat, welcomed with a cold drink, and your jacket is put away for you. I used to feel bad for those in the economic class as they had no idea what wonderful service we were receiving behind those curtains. I often wondered why they never let anyone see what they were giving to first-class passengers. We had traveled economic class for many years and only dreamed of one day being able to afford first-class tickets.

On this loyalty program, we get promoted frequently with our Sky Miles. I received all the wonderful service and ordered whatever meals I wanted, with a comfortable seat that turned into a comfortable bed. It felt like paradise, especially since I would be on that flight for more than twelve hours.

As I was enjoying everything, suddenly, I was no longer impressed with being in first-class. I wondered what went wrong; I was still receiving the same services from the very kind flight attendant, but I had no one to talk to. The one with whom I typically shared this pleasure was not with me. My husband, my lover, was what was missing. There was no one to enjoy this wonderful moment with me. I was with people, but they were all strangers and not my love. I was receiving joy, but I was not receiving the pleasure of *sharing* my joy.

Then the Holy Spirit began to minister to me from this feeling of "missing." The Father has all the glory of heaven and all the beauty of heaven, yet He stoops down to the earth to find you because he is longing for the pleasure of your companionship. His joy gets fuller with his children by His side, enjoying the riches of heaven with Him.

The Father wants you to have and enjoy life! For you to enjoy Him, and for Him to enjoy you.

> *"The Father has all the glory of heaven, and all the beauty of heaven, yet He stoops down to the earth to find you, because he is longs for the pleasure of your companionship."*

The Father has promoted you to first-class not just for the goodies and comfort you get to enjoy along the trip, but because He is the Captain, and He flies first-class. He wants you in the seat right next to him so that he can see your radiant eyes and enjoy the joy of you caring for and all your needs.

I always look forward to traveling with my beloved husband. The long hours on the plane are usually the longest time where I get to have his undivided attention. No children, no phone calls, no visitors, no ministry. It's so wonderful having him all to myself. I am relaxed with no need to cook or worry about the dishes. It is in these moments that we get to bond even deeper, and our love grows stronger. This is when the environment is set for heart-to-heart discussions, planning and dreaming together for the future.

The Heavenly Father also longs for that time when He can have your undivided attention, just you and Him for a sustained period of time. He wants a heart-to-heart talk: A Father-daughter date or a Father-son date with you.

It is in these moments that your heart gets attached to the Father's heart, and your thoughts get flooded with His thoughts. Your imagination gets locked into things above and not things on earth, and your affection is for Him alone.

A newborn baby belongs to the father and mother, but the child does not automatically bond to the parents. The parents are automatically attached to the child because they have been planning and talking and investing time and energy into the child for over nine months. At birth, the child could go home with anybody, not knowing the difference between a stranger and his/her parents. But as the child spends time with the father and mother, the child begins to cling to them and form strong attachments. It becomes difficult to separate or take the child from the parents.

The Heavenly Father is already attached to you because He had you on his mind from the foundations of the earth; He has been dreaming about you and has good plans for you. He has you engraved you in the palm of His hand.

Now is your turn to strengthen your bond with the Father by spending time to get to know Him.

Acknowledge Him in all your ways and authorize Him to direct your path like the widow collecting empty vessels, so that the Father can pour His everlasting love into you. The Father's love will spill over to your surroundings and bring life to all who pass by. This love will become so strong like mighty waters, and it will drive away all fear, all evil and all darkness. Amen.

AFTERWORD

"For God so loved the world, that he gave his only begotten Son, that whosoever believeth in him should not perish, but have everlasting life."

(John 3:16 KJV)

It is important for us to understand the power of love. When a child is born, the greatest longing of that child is to be loved. There's a craving to be appreciated and accepted in the heart of every human being. As you have read in the book, my wife was crying out for love. But I have good news! Jesus is our Lover.

Rejection is the feeling that you are not loved, and the Word of God has an answer, and the answer is the love of God! The love of God is the healing for rejection, being that you are loved by the One who owns the universe! The One who created everything around you! Whether you are accepted by man, your parents, your friends or anybody - it does not matter anymore!

So, my question for you today is *"Are you in love with Jesus? Have you met Jesus?"* Because dear reader, the day you meet true love, you will stop longing for it.

The Bible says very clearly that God is our husband. He is the One who loves us and who will NEVER, NEVER fail. Your mother may fail you, or siblings may fail you, but the love of God is BEYOND failure.

We are all longing for the desire of the ages, which is something in the heart of man that he desires. You may not accept the fact that He is your God. You may reject it. You may be fighting the longing in your heart and mind; suffering through the emptiness that nothing [else] can fill. But I'm encouraging you today to surrender to Him, and to accept TRUE LOVE. Your desires will be met, and you will begin to understand the goodness of God! You will begin to appreciate life and your future, and you will never be the same again.

Just as I met Him over 30 years ago, my life was transformed forever. Encounter Jesus, He is the answer to freedom from the Spirit of Rejection.

Pray with me:

Father of our Lord Jesus Christ, I thank you for Jesus. I thank You for the fact that You died for my sins. I receive Jesus as my Lord and Savior, and I surrender to the Lord Jesus Christ. I proclaim that Jesus is my love and the Answer to the longing of my heart. Lord Jesus, from my heart, forgive my sins. Wash me from all my sins. From today, I accept Jesus as my Lord and Savior. I am born again. My sins are gone. My names are written in the Book of Life. I am saved. Thank You Lord Jesus for saving me! Give me the power to serve You and follow You all the days of my life. In Jesus' name. Amen.

Bishop Robinson Fondong

Senior Pastor, CMFI Miracle Center USA

About the Author

Her spirit of joy is infectious, tangible and liberating!

Her fragrance goes before her and welcomes every living soul as family.

Her obedience makes a home for the homeless.

She loves with abandon and has an endless heart to serve.

Armed with and endowed by the fire, gentleness, and professorship of the Holy Spirit, Dr. Liz travels the globe ministering the Gospel of Jesus Christ. Going wherever the Lord sends her, Dr. Liz (so affectionately called) has ministered in different countries and at many conferences alongside her earthly king & husband, Bishop Robinson Fondong, of CMFI Miracle Center - USA in Westminster, Maryland.

She is the mother of 4 precious children and is the personification of the woman in Proverbs 31:28. The aroma and reach of her fruit extend beyond her family and nourishes hungry hearts, compelling them to the feet of the Father, to discover their own beauty and value and live their identity in Christ our Lord!

Dr. Liz promotes healing and wellness in her calling & professional career as a Doctor of Natural Medicine, as the founder of Hope Natural Medicine & Wellness Center and Owner of Harvestin' Natural located in Downtown Westminster, Maryland. She is also the founder and president of Arise and Shine Women's Ministry, an organization created to maximize potential in women and promote community development through corporate outreach.

Dr. Elizabeth Fondong, CNM, PhD, CFMP, is a surrendered, willing, and open vessel of God. She is in love with, and mentored by, Jesus Christ and she is dressed in the beautiful clothes of the Holy Spirit!

You can connect with Dr. Liz online at cmfimiraclecenter.com or via email at drlizfondongministries@gmail.com.

~Biography written by Jaz~

Made in the USA
Coppell, TX
23 September 2023

21892650R10083